Every Child Matters

This essential and ground-breaking resource for all practising and aspiring teaching assistants brings together all the crucial information necessary to support the full diversity of learners, from Early Years to Key Stage 4 in one comprehensive volume. Based on the revised National Occupational Standards for Supporting Teaching and Learning, this book effectively supports the personalised learning and *Every Child Matters* (ECM) well-being of children and young people in schools.

Coverage includes:

- An overview of the *Every Child Matters: Change for Children* programme and how this informs the role of the teaching assistant working in multi-disciplinary school personalised learning and well-being teams.
- Applying existing practical strategies to develop children and young people's skills as confident, collaborative and independent learners who experience positive ECM outcomes.
- Monitoring and evaluating the impact of teaching assistant support in improving the ECM outcomes.
- How teaching assistants can meet the requirements of the Ofsted inspection process.

This accessible, user-friendly book provides a wealth of practical resources, including photocopiable materials, templates and positive solution-focused advice to support busy teaching assistants.

Every Child Matters: A Practical Guide for Teaching Assistants provides a clear description of what the ECM agenda means for TAs and how it will impact on their role. It is also a valuable resource for all those line managing and supporting the continuing professional development of teaching assistants, from local authorities, Further Education and Higher Education organisations.

Rita Cheminais is the School Improvement Adviser for Inclusive Education in Tameside Services for Children and Young People.

Every Child Matters

A Practical Guide for Teaching Assistants

RITA CHEMINAIS

First published 2008
by Routledge
2 Park Square, Milton Park, Abingdon, Oxon OX14 4RN

Simultaneously published in the USA and Canada
by Routledge
270 Madison Ave, New York, NY 10016

Routledge is an imprint of the Taylor & Francis Group, an informa business

© 2008 Rita Cheminais

Typeset in Sabon by Wearset Ltd, Boldon, Tyne and Wear
Printed and bound in Great Britain by Bell & Bain Ltd, Glasgow

British Library Cataloguing in Publication Data
A catalogue record for this book is available from the British Library

Library of Congress Cataloging in Publication Data
A catalog record for this book has been requested

ISBN10: 0-415-45876-5 (pbk)
ISBN10: 0-203-46274-2 (ebk)

ISBN13: 978-0-415-45876-4 (pbk)
ISBN13: 978-0-203-46274-4 (ebk)

Contents

List of Figures and Tables

Figures

Tables

Acknowledgements

Thanks are due to colleagues throughout the country whom I have been privileged to meet while on my travels to a number of local authorities, who have highlighted the urgent need to produce a practical resource for all teaching assistants in schools outlining the implications of the *Every Child Matters: Change for Children* programme, in preparing them more effectively for their role in supporting pupils personalised learning and well-being.

Special thanks go to:

all the teaching assistants and teachers I have worked with in schools, who have helped me to identify the essential knowledge, skills and understanding TAs require in relation to improving personalised learning and well-being outcomes for the pupils they work with;

all the officers and colleagues in Tameside Services for Children and Young People who have continued to support my ideas and creativity;

Philip Eastwood, Advanced Skills Teacher for Initial Teacher Training in Knowsley local authority, who continues to inspire me to write practical books for those working within the Learning and Well-being school team;

last, but not least, Tracey Riseborough and Theresa Best, my previous two commissioning editors with David Fulton Publishers, and Routledge Taylor & Francis, who both encouraged and supported my work, and provided invaluable guidance in making this book a reality.

While every effort has been made to acknowledge sources throughout the book, such is the range of aspects covered that I may have unintentionally omitted to mention their origin. If so, I offer my apologies to all concerned.

The Aim of this Book

The aim of this book is to enable all teaching assistants (TAs) working in primary and secondary schools, regardless of their pupil remit within and outside the classroom, to reflect on their role within the current educational context, with particular reference to the *Every Child Matters* agenda and the revised National Occupational Standards for TAs, in order to know:

- what their role and expectations are in light of being a valuable member of the school learning and well-being team;
- how to remove barriers to achievement in supporting pupils personalised learning;
- how to support pupils in achieving positive *Every Child Matters* well-being outcomes;
- how to promote productive partnership working with teachers and other paraprofessionals;
- how to monitor and self-review the impact of their support on pupils learning and well-being outcomes, aligned to the Ofsted inspection framework and the school self-evaluation form.

Who the book is for

- school leaders and managers developing TAs capacity to meet the *Every Child Matters* agenda, the personalised learning and extended school initiatives;
- all teaching assistants contributing to transforming school learning communities for children and young people in the twenty-first century;
- class and subject teachers who want to ensure that they deploy teaching assistants effectively in order to maximise pupils' learning and well-being outcomes;
- all those from local authorities, FE and HE organisations responsible for training, and supporting the continuing professional development of all TAs working within schools;
- all those frontline practitioners from education, health and social care services who are working in partnership with teaching assistants in schools.

How the format is designed to be used

The book provides a resource that can be used:

- to act as a point of quick reference for aspiring and experienced teaching assistants in schools;
- to inform a more responsive consistent approach to supporting the *Every Child Matters* well-being outcomes and promoting personalised learning;
- to enable pages to be photocopied for development purposes, within the purchasing institution or service.

Abbreviations

AfL	assessment for learning
BESD	behavioural, emotional and social difficulties
BIP	Behaviour Improvement Programme
BSF	building schools for the future
CAF	Common Assessment Framework
CAMHS	Child and Adolescent Mental Health Services
CD	compact disc
CPD	continuing professional development
CWDC	Children's Workforce Development Council
CWN	Children's Workforce Network
CYPP	Children and Young People's Plan
DBERR	Department for Business, Enterprise and Regulatory Reform
DCSF	Department for Children, Schools and Families
DDA	Disability Discrimination Act
DFES	Department for Education and Skills
DH	Department of Health
DIUS	Department for Innovation, Universities and Skills
DME	dual or multiple exceptionality
DOB	date of birth
DVD	digital versatile disc
ECM	*Every Child Matters*
EHWB	emotional health and well-being
EWO	education welfare officer
FE	further education
FS	Foundation Stage
FSM	free school meals
GCSE	General Certificate of Secondary Education
HE	higher education
HLTA	higher level teaching assistant
ICT	information and communications technology
IIP	Investors in People
IM	instant messaging
INSET	in-service education and training
ISP	internet service provider
LA	local authority
LAC	looked after children
LDD	learning difficulties and/or disabilities
LGNTO	Local Government National Training Organisation
LSA	learning support assistant

MI	multiple intelligence
NCH	National Children's Homes
NHSS	National Healthy School Standard
NOS	National Occupational Standards
NSF	National Service Framework
NVQ	National Vocational Qualifications
Ofsted	Office for standards in education
PASS	Pupil Attitudes to Self and School
PDA	personal digital assistant
PE	Physical Education
PSHE	Personal, Social and Health Education
QTS	Qualified Teacher Status
RE	Religious Education
SEAL	Social and Emotional Aspects of Learning
SEBS	Social, Emotional and Behavioural Skills
SEF	self-evaluation form
SEN	special educational needs
SENCO	special educational needs coordinator
SMSC	spiritual, moral, social and cultural
SWDB	School Workforce Development Board
TA	teaching assistant
TDA	Training and Development Agency for Schools
UK	United Kingdom
UNICEF	United Nations International Children's Emergency Fund
UPN	unique pupil number
VAK	visual, auditory, kinaesthetic

Introduction

Schools in the twenty-first century are undergoing significant changes as they begin to embed *Every Child Matters* (ECM), personalised learning, extended school initiatives and transform learning communities through building schools for the future (BSF). All teaching assistants (TAs), as members of the whole school staff support team, working within this rapidly changing educational context, now and in the future, need to be at the cutting edge of these developments, in order to continue to further improve the learning and ECM well-being outcomes for children and young people in primary and secondary schools.

The DfES (2000) in *Working with Teaching Assistants: A Good Practice Guide* indicated that effective teaching assistant practice included: 'Fostering the participation of pupils in the social and academic practices of a school' (p.10), 'Seeking to enable pupils to become more independent learners' (p.11), and 'Help to raise standards of achievement of all pupils' (p.12).

The general role of the TA is to work under the direct instruction of teaching/senior staff, usually in the classroom, to support access to learning for pupils and provide general support to the teacher in the management of pupils and the classroom.

This general TA role focuses on four areas of support:

1 Support for pupils – promoting their inclusion and acceptance, their self-esteem and independence, ensuring their safety and access to learning, and acting as a positive role model.
2 Support for teachers – assisting in managing pupil behaviour; in keeping pupil records; undertaking routine administrative support tasks, e.g. filing and photocopying; assisting in preparing and tidying the classroom for lessons; displaying pupils' work; supporting the planning of learning activities.
3 Support for the curriculum – adjusting activities to match pupil needs and responses; interpret instructions for pupils; support the delivery of programmes linked to local and national strategies; support pupils in using ICT in learning activities.
4 Support for the school – appreciate and support the role of other professionals; assist in the provision of extended school activities; accompany teaching staff and pupils on educational visits; attend relevant meetings; contribute to the overall ethos, work and aims of the school; comply with school policies and procedures relating to child protection, health, safety, equal opportunities, confidentiality and data protection.

The number of teaching assistants has risen dramatically over the last ten years from 61,300 in 1997 to 152,800 in 2007, and continues to increase. The role of the teaching assistant has further developed and transformed over the last decade as an outcome of workforce remodelling, resulting in them becoming far more directly involved in supporting pupils learning and well-being, as opposed to being merely an extra pair of hands in the classroom.

Teaching assistants make a valuable contribution to children and young people's learning experiences, as members of the whole school Personalised Learning and Well-being Team. *Every Child Matters: Change for Children in Schools* (DfES 2004e) identified that pupil performance and well-being go hand in hand. Children and young people cannot learn effectively if they do not feel safe or if health problems create barriers.

Teaching assistants, as a result of supporting the development of the whole child and young person to achieve the five *Every Child Matters* outcomes of:

- being healthy
- staying safe
- enjoying and achieving
- making a positive contribution
- achieving economic well-being

are helping to remove barriers to achievement and to personalise learning to meet the full diversity of learners' needs.

Teaching assistants, like teachers, will become facilitators, enablers and promoters of pupils personalised learning and well-being, whereby pupils will achieve their optimum potential through learning in a way that suits them. This will entail teaching assistants in helping pupils of all abilities to acquire the skills and tools for learning: to develop into independent learners as well as cooperative learners, to raise learners expectations and aspirations, and to tackle and address 'coasting' learners.

Every Child Matters supports the principle of personalised learning by strengthening the focus on the impact of teaching assistant support on pupil outcomes.

Enhanced role for teaching assistants supporting teaching and learning in schools

Transforming learning communities through extended schools, building schools for the future, and personalisation will require teaching assistants to be:

- facilitators and enablers of pupils personalised learning, ensuring that support is tailored and matched to learners' individual needs;
- promoters of pupils inclusion by removing barriers to learning and participation in ensuring learners fulfil their optimum potential, and teaching and learning is strengthened;
- relationship builders and mediators between pupils, teachers and other significant adults responsible for children and young people's learning and well-being in the school learning community;
- enhancers of curriculum provision through offering a diverse range of skills and expertise as part of the extended school services and out of school hours learning activities and clubs;
- promoters of pupils' health and well-being by ensuring pupils are supported in an emotionally intelligent learning environment;
- dynamic key members of the school's multi-disciplinary learning and well-being team, working collaboratively in partnership with other paraprofessionals such as health and social care workers to improve ECM outcomes for children and young people;
- coaches and mentors to pupils and staff in school, in order to transfer knowledge and skills to help progress and improve pupils' learning and achievements;
- flexible, solution-focused problem solvers enabling pupils to manage and cope with change and choice in relation to their learning and well-being.

The review of the National Occupational Standards (NOS) for supporting teaching and learning in the classroom for teaching assistants, and the revision of support staff training to develop common core skills and knowledge for all who work with children, young people and families, as part of building the wider school workforce team to support learning, are positive national developments in preparing teaching assistants for their new and changing role.

Teaching assistants, as valuable members of the school workforce, need to be sufficiently well-trained and confident to meet this new agenda, in adapting and tailoring their support provision in order to remove any barriers that may prevent all pupils from successfully achieving the *Every Child Matters* outcomes.

Every teaching assistant matters because they play a crucial role in improving the *Every Child Matters* outcomes for children and young people they work with. Teaching assistants also enable the pupils they support to reach their optimum potential, within and beyond the classroom, as lifelong learners of the future.

This book will help to raise the profile of teaching assistants working as part of the school's Personalised Learning and Well-being Team. It provides all aspiring, newly appointed and experienced teaching assistants with practical guidance and strategies for supporting pupils in meeting each of the five ECM outcomes. The resource also signposts teaching assistants to further sources of information, in order to enable them to meet their new and exciting role in schools and other educational settings of the twenty-first century.

Every Child Matters: Opportunities and Challenges for Teaching Assistants

The origin and development of *Every Child Matters*

Every Child Matters (ECM), and the Children Act of 2004, was prompted by the tragic death of Victoria Climbié, and the many other children in England and Wales, who are at risk of, or die as a result of, abuse and neglect. *Every Child Matters* aims to protect, nurture and improve the life chances and well-being outcomes of all children and young people, in particular, of those who are the most disadvantaged and vulnerable. Table 1.1 outlines the development of *Every Child Matters* policy and legislation.

Children and young people cannot learn effectively if they do not feel safe or if health problems create barriers to their learning and well-being. Inclusion, ECM and educational achievement go hand in hand, and TAs as valuable members of the school's Children's Workforce team, play a crucial role in supporting teaching and learning, and removing barriers to learning and participation, in improving outcomes for all pupils, but particularly for those who are not succeeding in achieving the ECM outcomes.

The principles of *Every Child Matters*

Ten principles underpin the *Every Child Matters: Change for Children* programme.

- children to fulfil their optimum potential;
- early intervention and prevention through improved service provision;
- safeguarding and protecting children from harm, neglect and poverty;
- a well-trained, skilled, knowledgeable and flexible children's workforce;
- improving information sharing between agencies;
- better coordinated joined up integrated front-line services;
- greater accountability – impact of provision on outcomes for children and young people;
- children to voice their views and inform decision-making in relation to personalised services and personalised learning;
- safer communities providing recreational and voluntary activities for children and young people to participate in;
- improved access to advice, information and services for parents, carers and families on positive parenting, family learning, childcare, adoption and fostering.

Table 1.1 The development of *Every Child Matters*

Date	*Every Child Matters* developments
September 2003	Green Paper – Consultation document issued entitled: *Every Child Matters*. Document outlines the government's vision and proposals for improving services for all children and young people. It proposes the notion of a Lead Professional, responsible for coordinating a coherent package of services to meet a child's needs. Introduces the concept of developing a Common Assessment Framework (CAF), across services to support a more streamlined referral and intervention process. It described the changes the government wished to see taking place in local authorities (LAs), particularly the appointment of a Director of Children's Services, a Lead elected council member for Children's Services; Children's Trusts and a Local Safeguarding Children's Board established in each LA. The document outlined the developments it wished to see under Workforce Reform, in improving the skills, training and effectiveness of the Children's Workforce supporting improved service delivery and the achievement of the *Every Child Matters* five outcomes.
March 2004	*Every Child Matters: Next Steps* document published to coincide with the Children Bill. This described the government's next steps, following consultation from the Green Paper in September 2003, towards developing a programme of change for children and strengthening partnership working across services. It outlined the legislative steps for developing more accountable, effective and accessible services, focused around the needs of children, young people and their families in their local area. The National Service Framework (NSF) for Children, Young People and Maternity Services introduced a set of evidence-based standards for health, social care and some education services. The concept of Personalisation in learning, care and support was introduced. *Next Steps* set out a timetable for the implementation of the legislation in the Children Bill and the subsequent Children Act from 2004–2008.
November 2004	The Children Act 2004 becomes law and establishes: • a Children's Commissioner to champion the views and interests of children and young people; • a duty on key agencies to safeguard and promote the welfare of children; • a duty on LAs to set up Local Safeguarding Children Boards; • LAs to produce a Children and Young People's Plan (CYPP); • a duty on LAs to appoint a Director of Children's Services and a Lead Member for Children's Services; • the provision of indexes/databases containing basic information about children and young people for improved information sharing; • the creation of an integrated inspection framework for reviewing and assessing LA Children's Services progress in improving the five outcomes for children, young people and their families.
December 2004	*Every Child Matters: Change for Children* issued with four accompanying documents related specifically to expected changes in Schools, Social Care, Criminal Justice System and Health Services. *Change for Children* confirmed the national framework for local change programmes necessary for building better services around the needs of children and young people. It also emphasised the importance of listening to the views of children, young people and their families to inform service planning and improved service delivery. The *Every Child Matters* Outcomes Framework was published (Version 2 in September 2005), which was central to informing the 150 LAs change programmes. Download from website: www.everychildmatters.gov.uk/_files/16EE5ADDD79458F67747C0706D7AE742.pdf

The *Every Child Matters* five outcomes

The five *Every Child Matters* outcomes are interdependent and show the important link between educational achievement and well-being. They were identified by children and young people during consultation. The five outcomes that are key to well-being in childhood and later life are to:

- be healthy: enjoying good physical and mental health and having a healthy lifestyle;
- stay safe: being protected from harm and abuse;
- enjoy and achieve: getting the most out of life and developing the skills for adulthood;
- make a positive contribution: being involved with the community and society and not engaging in anti-social or offending behaviour;
- achieve economic well-being: not being prevented by economic disadvantage from achieving their full potential in life.

Each outcome is underpinned by five specific aims for children and young people, followed by a statement identifying the support needed from parents, carers and families in order to achieve those aims.

Key messages of *Every Child Matters*

Every Child Matters is all about improving the life chances of all children and young people, from birth to the age of 19, reducing inequalities, and helping them to achieve better outcomes.

The *Every Child Matters* five outcomes provide a deep moral basis for change for children in schools related to personalisation. This entails tailoring and matching support, teaching, learning and personalised services to meet individual needs, interests and aptitudes, in order to enable every child and young person to succeed within an education system fitting for the twenty-first century.

Every Child Matters (2003) and the government's *Five Year Strategy for Children and Learners* (2004), both set high aspirations for children and young people's outcomes in the future. The *Five Year Strategy* reiterated many of the key themes of *Every Child Matters*:

- a stronger voice for children, young people and adults in the development of policy and the design of services;
- services and learning designed around the needs of the individual and available at a time and place and in a form which suits their needs, with no artificial distinctions made between good learning and children's well-being;
- better advice and information to enable people to make choices;
- better support and incentives, particularly where financial barriers would work as a disincentive to participation;
- high minimum standards for everyone, irrespective of who they are or where they live.

(DfES 2004b: 13–14)

Every Child Matters clearly relates to, and underpins other key developments in education, as outlined in the DfES *Five Year Strategy for Children and Learners* (2004), and summarised in Table 1.3.

The key ECM messages in the transformation of the standards and quality of education and training, and services for children and families as identified in the *Five Year Strategy for Children and Learners* (2004) are to:

Table 1.2 *Every Child Matters* outcomes for children and young people

ECM outcome	ECM aims	Ofsted evidence
Be healthy	Physically healthy Mentally and emotionally healthy Sexually healthy Healthy lifestyles Choose not to take illegal drugs Parents, carers and families promote healthy choices	Regular exercise taken, including five hours' PE, sport per week Make informed healthy lifestyle choices Understand sexual health risks, the dangers of smoking and substance abuse Eat and drink healthily Recognise the signs of personal stress and develop strategies to manage it
Stay safe	Safe from maltreatment, neglect, violence and sexual exploitation Safe from accidental injury and death Safe from bullying and discrimination Safe from crime and anti-social behaviour in and out of school Have security, stability and are cared for Parents, carers and families provide safe home and stability	Display concern for others and refrain from intimidating and anti-social behaviour Feel safe from bullying and discrimination Feel confident to report bullying and racist incidents Act responsibly in high-risk situations Physical activities undertaken in an orderly and sensible manner
Enjoy and achieve	Ready for school Attend and enjoy school Achieve stretching national educational standards at primary school Achieve personal and social development and enjoy recreation Achieve stretching national educational standards at secondary school Parents, carers and families support learning	Have positive attitudes to education Behave well Have a good school attendance record Enjoy their learning very much Good personal development evidenced by high self-esteem High aspirations and increasing independence Make good progress in their learning
Make a positive contribution	Engage in decision-making and support the community and environment Engage in law-abiding and positive behaviour in and out of school Develop positive relationships and choose not to bully and discriminate Develop self-confidence and successfully deal with significant life changes and challenges Develop enterprising behaviour Parents, carers and families promote positive behaviour	Understand their legal and civil rights and responsibilities Show social responsibility and refrain from bullying and discrimination Able to express their views at school and are confident their views and 'voice' will be heard Involved in school and community activities
Achieve economic well-being	Engage in further education, employment or training on leaving school Ready for employment Live in decent homes and sustainable communities Access to transport and material goods Live in households free from low income Parents, carers and families are supported to be economically active	Develop basic skills in literacy, numeracy and ICT Develop their self-confidence and team working skills Become enterprising, and able to handle change in their lives Take initiative and calculate risk when making decisions Become financially literate and gain an understanding of business and the economy and of their career options Develop knowledge and skills when they are older, related to workplace situations

Table 1.3 Five-year strategy for children and learners and ECM outcomes

Aims of five year strategy for children and learners	ECM outcomes	Examples of developments
Every child to get the best possible start in life – with integrated services focused on the needs of parents and children	All five ECM outcomes	Children's centres providing childcare, education, health, employment and parenting support More flexible pre-school 'educare'
Every primary school to offer high standards in the basics in the context of a broad, rich and enjoyable curriculum	Enjoy and achieve	High quality teacher and support staff in classrooms giving children more tailored learning, with opportunities to make best possible progress in reading, writing and maths Every child able to learn a foreign language, play music and take part in competitive sport Increased family learning opportunities More primary schools working together in networks to support each other
Every secondary school to offer excellent teaching, an exciting curriculum, and a positive and attractive environment	Enjoy and achieve	Reduced curriculum prescription, with catch up in English and Maths, and stretch for all pupils Use of leading edge technology to support learning Every school able to become a specialist school as a centre of curriculum excellence Academies as new schools Every secondary school to be refurbished or rebuilt as part of BSF Secondary schools able to form foundation partnerships to address issues such as hard to place pupils, SEN, together between schools
All schools acting as community 'hubs' to become healthy schools, inclusive schools, and enterprising schools (with real links to business)	Be healthy Enjoy and achieve Make a positive contribution Achieve economic well-being	All schools, as universal service providers, becoming extended schools, offering a core of services on the site of the school, or across a group of schools, in a local area
At 14–19, every young person to have a personalised pathway to suit them that fits them for work, further learning, and for life as an adult; and a wide range of activities outside school or college to enjoy and take part in	Enjoy and achieve Make a positive contribution Achieve economic well-being	Introduction of Diplomas at three levels: 1(Foundation), 2(GCSE) and 3(advanced) in 14 occupational lines of learning Greater vocational opportunities for work-based learning and apprenticeships More choice of where to study
Every child and young person who is in difficult circumstances to get the extra support they need without stigma	All five ECM outcomes	Access to extra support for young people leaving care (LAC) High quality advice and guidance to help young people make good decisions – Connexions Personal Advisers, 'learning guides' in schools
Adult learners to all get and build the skills they need for success in employment – because employers are in the lead in designing and delivering training, working with highly responsive colleges	Achieve economic well-being	High quality FE courses and HE courses Free tuition for adults learning basic skills Adult Learning Grants for those going for Level 2 qualifications – (equivalent to 5 good GCSEs)

- achieve and sustain world class excellence in every part of the system;
- move further towards early intervention and work to prevent problems;
- create services which are truly personalised around the needs and aspirations of every child, young person and adult; and
- put learning – and the high quality workforce and institutions needed to provide it – at the heart of successful communities and local and regional regeneration.

(DfES 2004b: 11:16)

In the follow up to the *Five Year Strategy* (2006f) the government remarked:

> Personalised learning, the reform of 14–19 qualifications and provision, the development of the children's centres and extended schools … and the revolution in children's services following *Every Child Matters* and the Children Act 2004, have all pointed the way forward. These programmes have reconfigured services across traditional boundaries to create provision that is shaped around the user's needs.
>
> (DfES 2006f: 33:81)

The DfES in the same document referred to a new framework for 'sustaining success', which builds on the *Every Child Matters* five outcomes, in setting objectives and expectations for good high quality services for children and young people.

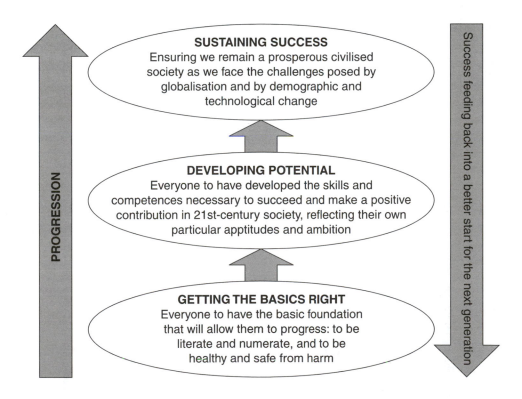

Figure 1.1 A framework for sustaining success in achieving the *Every Child Matters* outcomes. Source: DfES 2006f: 37.

Implications for teaching assistants in schools

The implications of *Every Child Matters* on the role of the teaching assistant supporting pupils learning and well-being in schools, can best be summarised in Table 1.4.

Table 1.4 ECM and implications for teaching assistants' roles

ECM principles	Implications for TA role
Children and young people to fulfil their optimum potential	**Facilitator and promoter of personalised learning** – supporting pupils as active learners to know how to learn, use their brain to best effect, and become independent and collaborative learners
Early intervention and prevention through improved service provision	**Analyst of data and information** – able to interpret pupil information and data to inform the nature and level of TA support required for learning and ECM well-being
Safeguarding and protecting children and young people from harm, neglect and poverty	**Supporter of pupils' welfare** – knowing the correct child protection and safeguarding procedures to follow, respecting confidentiality
A well trained, skilled, knowledgeable and flexible children's workforce	**Leader for own continuing professional development** – identifying ongoing training and support to meet changing role for ECM, including coaching and mentoring
Improving information sharing between agencies	**Champion for children** – following the correct data protection and information sharing protocols, to ensure that other professionals working with the pupils you support, target their provision appropriately, taking account of your information and knowledge about the pupil
Better coordinated joined-up integrated front-line services	**Collaborative partnership team worker** – TA making role explicit to other stakeholders/partners in the school's learning and well-being team, and the role of other front-line workers from health, social care and education being clear to the TA
Greater accountability in terms of knowing the impact of provision on the outcomes for children and young people	**Quality assuror** – Collecting and recording appropriate evidence to demonstrate the impact of TA support on improving pupils' learning and ECM well-being outcomes, which feeds into the school's self-evaluation form (SEF)
Children and young people able to voice their views and inform decision making in relation to personalised services and personalised learning	**Pupil advocate** – supporting pupils in an emotionally intelligent and trusting learning environment, where they feel safe to express their views about their learning, progress, well-being and TA support, in order to inform future personalised learning and ECM provision
Safer communities providing recreational and voluntary activities for children and young people to participate in	**Local community representative** – as a resident living within the pupils' local community, contribute your knowledge about what extended services and local recreational activities should be made available for children and young people in the local area
Improved access to advice, information and services for parents, carers and families	**Sharer and creator of knowledge** – contribute to up-dating and signposting parents/carers to further sources of information and help, in relation to them supporting their child's learning and well-being at home

Opportunities for TAs supporting learning and ECM outcomes

In the context of the *Every Child Matters: Change for Children* programme and personalised learning, the role of the TA necessitates reconfiguration and reconceptualisation, in order to better equip teaching assistants fully to meet the new and exciting opportunities in schools of the future.

Figure 1.2 illustrates comprehensively the new opportunities for the TA role.

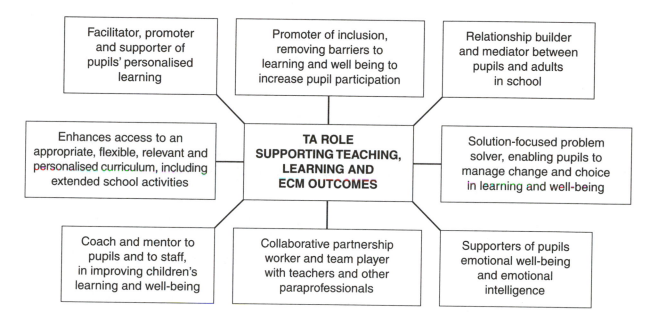

Figure 1.2 The teaching assistants' role in supporting the ECM outcomes.

Challenges for teaching assistants and *Every Child Matters*

Teaching assistants supporting teaching, learning and pupil well-being in schools in the twenty-first century will need to acquire new knowledge, skills and understanding to enable them to:

- support children and young people who may be less passive and biddable as learners of the future;
- become fully conversant with, and confident in using leading edge technology to support pupils' learning and promote self-directed learning;
- refocus support to enable pupils to know how to learn, how to use their brains and become more effective learners;
- support pupils to become more active learners, taking greater ownership and responsibility for their learning, providing opportunities for them to talk about their learning and well-being;
- prepare for the role of a pupil 'learning guide' and advocate, who understands pupils' learning needs in the wider context, and establishes and reviews their learning needs, and monitors their progress;
- understand how children and young people develop, being aware of the adverse peer group and societal pressures they face, and help them to manage these competing pressures and their own emotions;

- help pupils develop 'soft' ECM skills: reliability, punctuality and perseverance; how to work with other peers in a team; how to evaluate information critically; how to develop effective learning habits; able to investigate and solve problems; be resilient to difficulties; and how to be creative, inventive and enterprising;
- support pupils in adopting a more solution-focused approach to assessing and reviewing their own progress in learning and well-being, and knowing what they need to do to improve in both aspects;
- knowing how to interpret and analyse pupil level data in learning and ECM well-being outcomes in order to inform and personalise future pupil support approaches;
- becoming conversant with the future curriculum developments and changes for the age group of pupils being supported;
- ensure a healthy work–life balance and manage time effectively by not taking on too many competing priorities.

Further activities for teaching assistants

The following questions on aspects covered in this chapter, are designed to promote further discussion and identify ways forward in enabling TAs to effectively meet the *Every Child Matters* agenda in schools.

- What is your own view of *Every Child Matters* in the context of the school you are currently working in?
- How will the *Every Child Matters* agenda influence and shape the future direction of your role as a teaching assistant?
- What role do you consider TAs should play in contributing to ensuring pupils achieve successful *Every Child Matters* outcomes?
- What opportunities does *Every Child Matters* offer to you in your TA role supporting teaching, learning and well-being?
- In what ways has your school already begun to involve and engage teaching assistants in the development and implementation of *Every Child Matters*, and the broader educational change agenda?
- What are the major challenges posed by *Every Child Matters* in relation to the role of teaching assistants in your school?
- How could these challenges be addressed, overcome and resolved in your school context?
- Who will be able to support you professionally within and outside school, in preparing to meet the *Every Child Matters* change for children programme?

2

Teaching Assistants Removing Barriers to Learning and Well-being

Introduction

Every Child Matters identifies that pupil performance and well-being go hand in hand. Children and young people cannot learn effectively if they feel unsafe, or if health problems create barriers.

Barriers to learning experienced by pupils in schools more often arise as a result of:

- an unsuitable learning environment;
- inappropriate pupil groupings;
- ineffective deployment of teaching assistants;
- a limited range of teaching styles being utilised;
- inaccessible curriculum materials; and
- inflexible timetabling and curriculum learning pathways.

Teaching assistants play a crucial role in helping to minimise and remove barriers to learning, achievement and participation, in order to enhance curriculum access, and enable pupils to achieve their optimum potential. Personalised learning that is responsive and tailored to the diverse needs of all learners, ensures that pupils are helped to learn, achieve and participate fully within inclusive classrooms, where the learning, achievements, attitudes and well-being of every pupil matter.

It is vital that teachers and teaching assistants, in partnership together, and with other paraprofessionals, play complementary roles in removing barriers to learning, and in focusing on the needs of the whole child and young person. This chapter will provide teaching assistants with a comprehensive overview of the concepts of personalised learning, assessment for learning, inclusion and productive partnerships. This will enable TAs to consider how these key concepts influence their support role.

Personalised learning

Personalised learning is an ongoing process linked to the *Every Child Matters* agenda, which helps to enhance the outcomes for all children and young people. It optimises learners' engagement and success through enhanced learning relationships. Central to personalised

Figure 2.1 Key factors supporting the removal of barriers to learning.

learning is every aspect of teaching and support being designed around a pupil's needs. Personalised learning is the process of tailoring and matching teaching and learning around the way different learners learn in order to meet individual needs, interests and aptitudes to enable every pupil to reach their optimum potential. *The 2020 Vision Report on Teaching and Learning* (2006), defined personalised learning as: 'taking a more structured and responsive approach to each child's learning, so that all pupils are able to progress, achieve and participate' (Teaching and Learning in 2002 Review Group 2006: 41).

The purpose of personalised learning is to promote personal development in pupils' through self-realisation, self-development and self-enhancement to become active, responsible, self-motivated lifelong learners.

The DfES (2004b), identified the essential features of pupils' personalised learning entitlement as comprising of:

- having pupils' individual needs addressed, both in schools and beyond the classroom, into the family and community;
- entailing coordinated support to enable pupils to succeed to the full, irrespective of their ability or background;
- providing a safe and secure learning environment, where learners problems are effectively addressed; and
- giving pupils a voice and choice about their learning.

The government in *Removing Barriers to Achievement: The Government's Strategy for SEN* (2004), commented:

We need to provide a personalised education that brings out the best in every child, that builds on their strengths, enables them to develop a love of learning; and helps them to grow into confident and independent citizens, valued for the contribution they make.

(DfES 2004a: 49)

In the same document, the government goes on to identify how teachers and teaching assistants can best deliver personalised learning:

- having high expectations
- building on the knowledge, interests and aptitudes of every child
- involving children in their own learning through shared objectives and feedback (assessment for learning)
- helping children to become confident learners
- enabling children to develop the skills they will need beyond school.

(ibid.: 52)

The DfES specified the five components of personalised learning as being:

- assessment for learning to utilise evidence and dialogue to identify every pupil's learning needs;
- effective teaching and learning to develop the competence and confidence of every learner to actively engage and 'stretch' them in the learning process;
- curriculum entitlement and choice to deliver breadth of study, personal relevance and flexible learning pathways;
- school as a learning organisation taking a pupil-centred approach to school organisation in order to support high quality teaching and personalised learning, i.e. building schools for the future around the needs of learners;
- beyond the classroom and school to remove barriers to learning and to support pupils well-being, i.e. improving *Every Child Matters* outcomes, and building positive relationships with the community and parents/carers.

Research into personalised learning in schools

The DfES commissioned researchers to investigate personalised learning approaches being used by schools in 2006. The final research findings were published in May 2007 in *An Investigation of Personalised Learning Approaches Used by Schools*, which concluded that the personalised learning initiatives having the greatest impact on attainment in schools were:

- genuine pupil voice and choice;
- assessment for learning;
- pupil self and peer assessment;
- target-setting;
- pupil tracking;
- pupils taking greater responsibility for their own learning;
- mentoring and coaching pupils;
- drawing on pupils' prior experiences in lessons;
- recognising the 'personal' in teaching and learning support;
- high level of pupil participation in learning to learn;
- focus on learning styles and thinking skills;
- vocational and alternative flexible curriculum pathways at KS4 and KS5;
- strong links with the community;

- reorganisation of teaching assistants, learning mentors and administrative staff to provide more flexible support to individual pupils and small groups who are underachieving or falling behind, which includes targeted interventions, i.e. 'catch-up' and 'stretch', booster classes.

Teaching assistants reviewing their support for personalised learning

In your role as a teaching assistant supporting pupils' personalised learning, reflect upon and respond to the following questions.

1 What personalised learning initiatives and activities have TAs been involved in within the school?
2 What has been the impact of the personalised learning approaches and strategies you have utilised in relation to improving pupils learning and *Every Child Matters* well-being outcomes?
3 Of all the personalised learning approaches and strategies you have used when supporting pupils learning, which **one** has had the greatest impact on raising pupils attainment and why?
4 Which group(s) of learners in school do you consider to have benefited the most from personalised learning approaches in school?
5 Are there any groups of learners in your school who are not benefiting from, or who are missing out on, personalised learning approaches to meet their needs?
6 In relation to the five components of personalised learning, in which one(s) would you welcome further professional development?
7 Is there anything else you wish to comment on in relation to the role of the teaching assistant in supporting pupils' personalised learning?

Figures 2.2 and 2.3 provide a useful checklist for TAs on the elements of personalised learning for each of the five components.

David Hargreaves identified nine interlinked gateways to the content of personalised learning. These reflect some of the DfES components and are illustrated in Figure 2.4.

Personalised learning supports the needs of the whole child and young person.

Implications of personalised learning on teaching assistants' roles

Using Figures 2.2 and 2.3 as points of reference, map aspects of your current role against the five components of personalised learning on Figure 2.5. This will help TAs to identify any aspects or areas related to supporting pupils' personalised learning that require further professional development, which can be discussed with their line manager at their next professional review meeting.

Further information about personalised learning can be found by accessing the following websites:

www.standards.dfes.gov.uk/personalisedlearning
www.standards.dfes.gov.uk/innovation-unit/personalisation

Assessment for learning

According to the Assessment Reform Group (2002):

> Assessment for learning is the process of seeking and interpreting evidence for use by learners and their teachers to decide where the learners are in their learning, where they need to go and how best to get there.

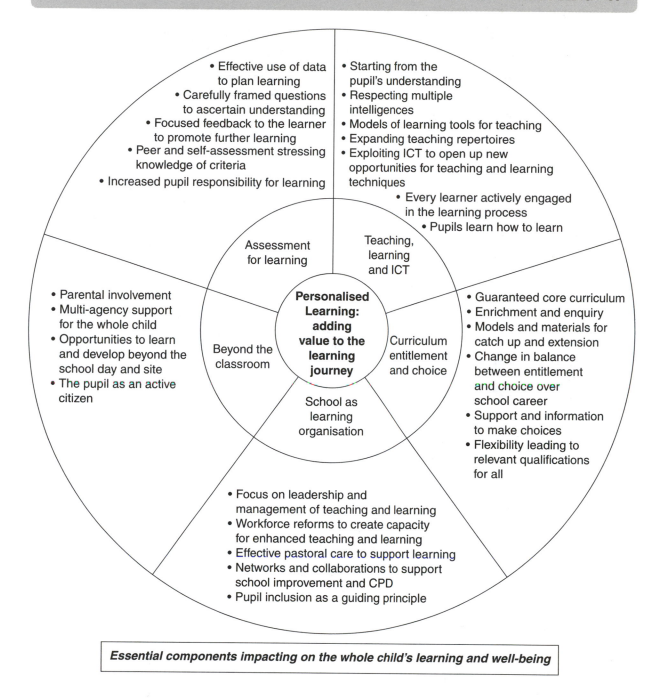

Figure 2.2 Personalised learning.

The Assessment Reform Group identified ten principles of assessment for learning (AfL) to guide classroom practice which will be of interest to TAs. Refer to: http://www.assessment-reform-group.org.uk to view these principles. Assessment for learning is effective when pupils:

- show positive changes in their attitudes to learning and in their motivation, self-esteem, independence, initiative and confidence;
- make positive responses and contributions to questions, plenary and discussion sessions, and in providing explanations and descriptions;
- improve their attainment;
- ask relevant questions;
- are actively involved in formative assessment processes, e.g. setting targets, peer or self-assessment, recognising progress in their written work, skills, knowledge and understanding.

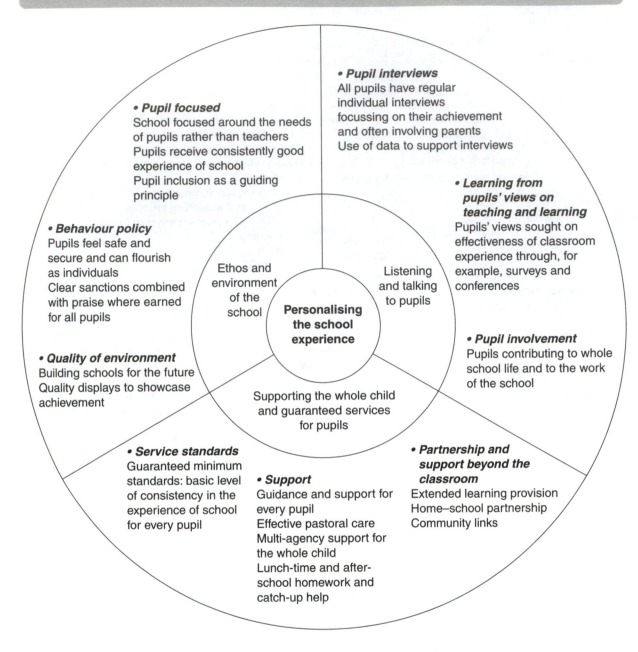

Figure 2.3 Personalising the learning experience: school organisation and beyond the classroom.

Like teachers, TAs when supporting and working with pupils, need to:

- help pupils to understand what they have done well and what they need to develop, and to admit task problems without risk to their self-confidence;
- know why pupils may make mistakes in their learning, and be able to offer supportive suggestions and feedback about possible next steps on how to improve;
- share learning intentions and expectations with pupils, so they know and recognise the standards to aim for;
- build in review time to assess pupils' learning and give pupils time to reflect on their own work;
- encourage pupils to take responsibility for their learning by providing opportunities for pupils to describe their response to learning intentions and targets, the learning strategies they use, and to judge their own progress;
- model good learning and assessment for learning approaches to pupils and show them examples of pupils work from other classes, so they know what is required;

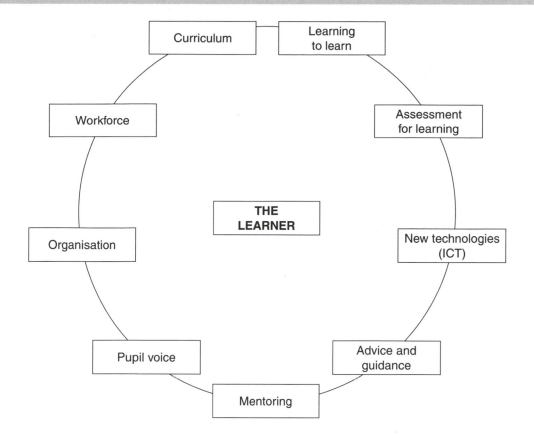

Figure 2.4 The nine gateways to personalising learning. Source: Hargreaves 2004: 7.

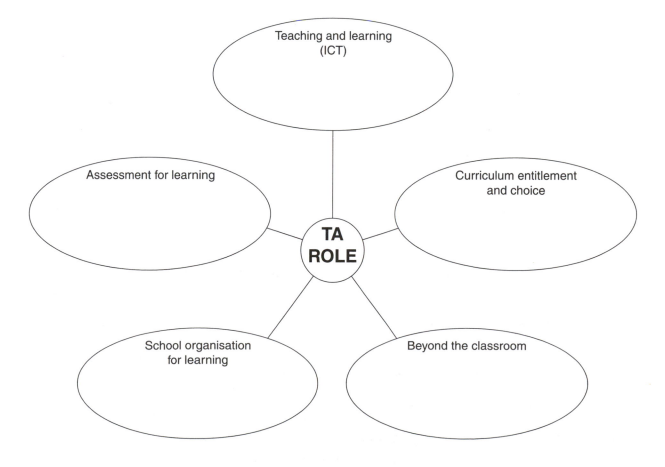

Figure 2.5 Teaching assistants mapping support to personalised learning.

- analyse pupils' performance and outcomes and use the information to inform future support for teaching, learning and pupil well-being;
- make note of any pupils who may need additional or consolidation work;
- note down what did or did not work with pupils and why;
- measure individual pupils against their own previous attainment, rather than comparing them with other pupils;
- promote trusting relationships that encourage pupils to assess and review their own learning and well-being outcomes with confidence;
- make good use of oral feedback as well as written feedback when assessing pupils' progress in learning;
- make use of high-level questioning as a tool for assessment for learning to find out what pupils know, understand and can do.

Examples of types of questions that support assessment opportunities are:

- how can we be sure that...?
- what is the same and what is different about...?
- is it ever/always true/false that...?
- how do you know...?
- how would you explain...?
- what does that tell us about...?
- what is wrong with...?
- why is ... true?

The revised NOS supporting teaching and learning in schools expects TAs to observe and report on pupil performance and contribute to assessment for learning. Table 2.1 provides a useful summary of the characteristics of AfL. The information on assessment for learning in this section of the chapter has been taken from the following websites:

www.qca.org.uk/printable.html?url=/296.html&title=CharacteristicsofAfL
www.qca.org.uk/printable.html?url=/295.html&title=AfLchecklist
www.assessment-reform-group.org

Inclusion for all learners

Inclusion is concerned about:

- the quality of a pupil's experience;
- providing access to a high quality education which enables pupils to make progress in their learning;
- how pupils are helped to learn, achieve and participate fully in the activities and life of their school and community.

The DfES in 2004 acknowledged that:

> Effective inclusion relies on more than specialist skills and resources. It requires positive attitudes towards children who have difficulties in schools, a greater responsiveness to individual needs and critically, a willingness among all staff to play their part.
>
> (DfES 2004a: 32, 2.7)

Inclusion, like personalised learning, is an ongoing process focused on the presence, participation and achievement of the full diversity of children and young people within the classroom and the school.

Table 2.1 Characteristics of assessment for learning

Key characteristics of AfL	Key developments for schools
AfL is embedded in a view of learning and teaching of which it is an essential part.	• Conditions for learning • Designing opportunities for learning • Day-to-day assessment strategies
AfL involves sharing learning goals with learners.	• Using curricular targets • Designing opportunities for learning • Feedback on learning
AfL aims to help learners to know and to recognise the standards for which they are aiming.	• Using curricular targets • Formative use of summative assessment
AfL involves learners in peer and self-assessment.	• Feedback on learning • Day-to-day assessment strategies • Formative use of summative assessment
AfL provides feedback which leads to learners recognising their next steps and how to take them.	• Feedback on learning • How ICT can be used to support AfL
AfL is underpinned by the confidence that every learner can improve.	• Conditions for learning • Feedback on learning
AfL involves both learner and teacher reviewing and reflecting on assessment data.	• Feedback on learning • Involving parents and carers • Formative use of summative assessment data • How ICT can be used to support AfL

Source: DfES 2004k: 10.

The concept of inclusion is based upon a set of guiding principles, whereby all children and young people, regardless of their ability, gender, language, ethnic or cultural origin are valued equally, treated with respect and provided with real opportunities in school.

The *Primary National Strategy* (DfES 2006e) identifies that inclusive teaching (and TA support):

* is set within a culture of high expectations for all learners;
* emphasises what a pupil will learn rather than the activities they will do;
* is based on an assessment of what the pupil already knows, can do and understands;
* uses teaching styles that meet the needs of individuals and groups so that all pupils are engaged in learning;
* establishes access strategies to help overcome potential barriers to learning taking place.

The strategy confirms that inclusive teaching and support for learning in the classroom ensures:

* teachers and TAs have high expectations of all learners, they are clear about the age-related expectations and about the individual needs and differences of pupils in their classes;
* pupils are clear about what they are learning and need to learn in order to make progress; learning objectives and success criteria are always made explicit, as are links within and between subject areas;
* assessment involves all the adults in the classroom and the pupils themselves; it is based on observation, questioning, listening and reflective responses, using summative assessment formatively;
* planning takes account of a range of learning and teaching styles and offers variety and choice in method and experience for pupils;
* the reason and purpose of different access strategies are shared with both the pupil and other adults working in the classroom.

(DfES 2006e: Inclusive teaching PowerPoint and presentation notes)

The *Key Stage 3 Strategy* (now the *Secondary Strategy*), indicated that inclusion:

- is about valuing the diversity and showing respect for all individuals;
- promotes equity and entitlement;
- is a collective, whole school responsibility, which requires effective tracking and monitoring of the progress of all pupils;
- requires individual teachers to think carefully about lesson design to ensure that barriers to learning are removed;
- concerns all groups of pupils who may be underperforming because their personalised learning needs are not being met.

(DfES 2004j: 5)

Both the primary and secondary national strategies make reference to the National Curriculum inclusion statement of principles illustrated in Figure 2.6. Irrespective of recent curriculum revisions, these inclusion principles are still relevant.

Inclusion takes a holistic approach to meeting the individual needs of pupils, and is reliant on the following essential characteristics:

- flexible curriculum provision;
- personalised learning and personalised services tailored to meet learners diverse needs;
- effective deployment of adult support;
- flexibility in the range of teaching approaches and teaching pupils how to learn;
- commitment to inclusion that is shared by all staff;
- careful assessment of assessment for learning;
- focus on outcomes for learners;
- an ethos of acceptance of all pupils.

Ofsted (2002), in their report on the evaluation of the quality and impact of teaching assistants' work, found TAs to be most successful and efficient in their support role when they have:

- an understanding of children and their needs and behaviour;
- an ability to interact with pupils to promote learning;
- an ability to assess where pupils are in their learning and what they need to do make further progress.

(Ofsted 2002: 18:65)

Implications of inclusion on the role of teaching assistants

Using Figure 2.7, map aspects of your current role against the three principles of inclusion illustrated in Figure 2.6. Identify any aspects of inclusive support practice where further professional development would be beneficial, and discuss these training needs with your line manager.

Further information about inclusion can be found on the following websites:

www.inclusion.ngfl.gov.uk

www.inclusive-solutions.com

www.standards.dfes.gov.uk/primary/publications/inclusion/1146355

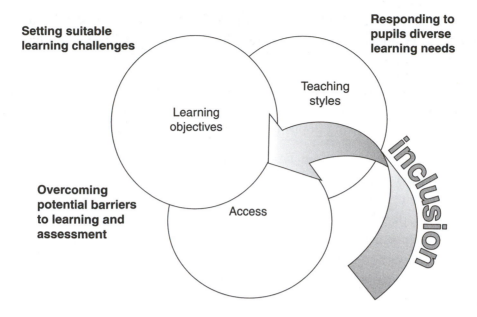

Figure 2.6 National Curriculum inclusion statement of principles for all pupils.

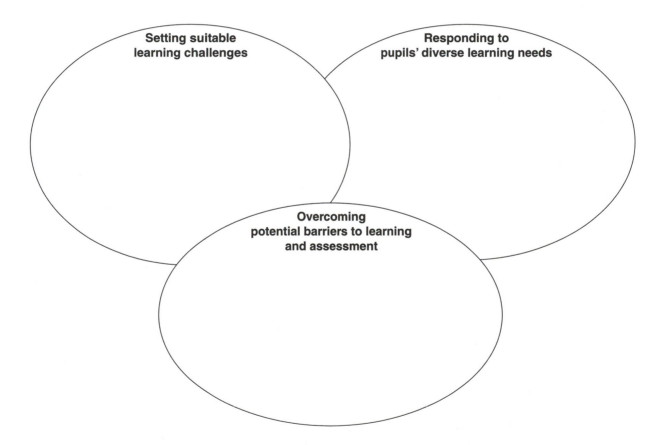

Figure 2.7 Teaching assistants mapping support role to inclusion principles.

Productive partnerships

The NOS for TAs to support teaching and learning in the classroom cover the TA role in relation to contributing to the development of effective teamwork through developing and maintaining working relationships with colleagues and other practitioners.

The concept of a partnership entails a group of people joining together, sharing a common problem or issue to be addressed, who all take collective responsibility for resolving it, i.e. improving ECM outcomes for pupils, and removing barriers to learning.

TAs, along with other supporting adults and professionals supporting pupils learning and well-being in school, share a common purpose of minimising barriers to learning, improving outcomes for pupils, and ensuring pupils fulfil their optimum potential.

Teachers value the contributions from TAs and other multi-agency, voluntary partners and professionals in removing barriers to learning, as this enables them to focus on their core role of teaching and learning. Evidence of effective multi-agency working in partnership with the schools staff who support learning and well-being is when, for example: 'social workers and therapists work together with teachers and teaching assistants to agree reasons for difficulties and to identify strategies to improve the progress the pupils make in their learning' (Ofsted 2004c: 13, 55). Teaching assistants, along with other professionals as partners from within and beyond the school, i.e. education, health and social care, are helping to develop the 'softer' skills among pupils which support the ECM outcomes. The 'softer' skills include:

- being able to communicate effectively orally;
- reliability, punctuality and perseverance;
- knowing how to work with others in a team;
- knowing how to evaluate information critically;
- taking responsibility for, and being able to manage, their own learning and developing the habits of effective learning;
- knowing how to work independently without close supervision;
- being confident;
- being able to investigate problems and find solutions;
- being resilient in the face of difficulties;
- being creative, inventive, enterprising and entrepreneurial.

(Teaching and Learning in 2020 Review Group 2006: 10)

Principles of partnership working

Effective partnership working is based on the three Cs:

- cooperation – partners sharing information and recognising the value of partnership working, i.e. pooling their collective knowledge, skills, expertise and achievements in supporting pupils' learning and well-being;
- coordination – partners plan together to focus on a specific ECM outcome, for example, sharing some roles and responsibilities, resources and safe risk-taking;
- collaboration – longer term commitment between partners, which brings some organisational change, workforce remodelling, shared leadership, resources, i.e. the formation of the school personalised learning and ECM well-being team.

Features of effective partnership working

- The aims, goals and key purpose of the partnership are clear.
- A common language and terminology is used and understood between TAs and other partners supporting pupils learning and well-being.
- Roles and responsibilities of all partners working with TAs are known by them, and vice versa, to avoid overlap and duplication of roles.

- Partnership working is based on relationships of trust, mutual respect, a shared sense of ownership and team work, and it is clear what each partner contributes.
- All partners supporting pupils' learning and well-being follow the correct procedures and protocols in relation to information sharing.
- Realistic expectations exist as to what the partnership can hope to achieve.
- Realistic agreed targets have been set for joint partnership working.
- Joint training between TAs and paraprofessionals supporting pupils in the school take place.
- Effectiveness and impact of partnership working is systematically monitored and evaluated.

Further activities for teaching assistants

The following questions on aspects covered in this chapter are designed to promote further discussion, and help to identify ways forward in enabling TAs to effectively target and tailor their support in partnership with other professionals, to meet the needs of pupils in inclusive schools.

- How will you ensure that you play an active role as a TA supporting personalised learning activities within the classroom?
- What support strategies work best with particular types of learners within the context of personalised learning?
- What further contributions could you realistically make as a TA to the personalised learning agenda in your school?
- How can you ensure that your support for the inclusion of pupils is clearly focused on establishing their presence, participation and achievement in learning and well-being?
- What does the concept of inclusion mean to you as a TA in the context of your own school?
- Do others in the learning and well-being team/school share the same understanding about inclusion?
- Inclusion works best in a culture of collaboration. In your current TA role, how are you working more effectively in partnership with teachers and other professionals to remove barriers to pupils' learning?
- How can you ensure that TA contributions relating to pupil progress towards meeting the ECM outcomes are fed into multi-agency pupil review meetings?
- What factors would enhance and further improve TA partnership working with other professionals from health, social care and education in the school?
- How could you be more effectively deployed within the school in respect of meeting the ECM agenda?
- Are the roles and responsibilities of teaching assistants in your school clearly defined and known by teachers and other partners?
- Are the roles and responsibilities of other partners from multi-agency and voluntary/community organisations clear to you?
- How are you contributing towards the assessment for learning of the pupils you support through observation and feedback to the class teacher and the pupil?
- How do you ensure that pupils transfer what they have learned with you in intervention and catch-up programmes, across the curriculum?

3

Every Child Matters and the Role of the Teaching Assistant

Support staff working in schools

Half a million support staff working in schools, of which 152,800 are teaching assistants, play an essential role in improving outcomes for children and young people in relation to promoting their learning, health and well-being. There are around 30 different types of support staff job roles in schools, that contribute to pupils achieving the five *Every Child Matters* outcomes. Some support staff may undertake two or more roles within a school, or between schools, for example, a teaching assistant may also work as a midday supervisor.

Table 3.1 lists the main categories of support work with examples of the range of support staff jobs undertaken in schools.

Several of these school support staff, and in particular teaching assistants and higher level teaching assistants (HLTAs), under workforce reform and remodelling, free up time for teachers in order to enable them to increase their focus on teaching and strengthen pupils' learning.

Support staff play an essential role in contributing to school improvement and inclusion, by making schools a more efficient, enriching educational environment for pupils. The role of schools is changing, and although they are still primarily concerned with pupils' educational achievement, increasingly they are working with other community services and with families to guarantee children and young people's well-being, and to help them reach their full potential.

The need for an increasingly highly skilled and flexible school workforce becomes crucial as schools embrace *Every Child Matters* and personalised learning; offer an increased range of extended services; increase their specialisation; and offer more choice for pupils and parents.

Teaching assistants, as part of the school support staff team, are already making a difference to many aspects of school life for children and young people, and the impact on children's attainment and well-being is clearly noticeable in the areas related to:

- support for learning within the classroom and in the delivery of catch-up and intervention programmes for literacy and numeracy;
- inclusion and achievement by encouraging and promoting positive behaviour, improved attendance and greater participation in learning by pupils;

Table 3.1 School support staff roles

School support staff categories	Examples of support staff job titles
Learning support	Nursery nurse, Early Years assistant, Foundation Stage assistant, Therapist; Teaching assistant, Learning support assistant, Bilingual support assistant, Language assistant; Higher level teaching assistant (HLTA); Special needs assistant; Cover assistant, supervisor or manager; Sports coach.
Pupil support for welfare and well-being	Learning mentor, Careers adviser, Connexions personal adviser, Education welfare officer (EWO), Home–school liaison officer; Welfare assistant; Health care assistant, School nurse; Midday supervisor, Play worker, Out-of-school care worker/manager, Extended school club worker/manager.
Specialist and technical support	ICT technician; Science technician, Laboratory technician, Design and technology technician, Food technology technician, Textiles technician, Art and Craft technician; Library assistant, Librarian.
Administrative support	Clerical assistant, Receptionist, Office manager, School business manager; Finance officer, Bursar; Examinations officer, Examinations invigilator, Examinations manager.
Catering support	Catering assistant, Assistant cook, Cook, Catering manager.
Site support	Cleaner, Caretaker, Premises supervisor, Site manager.

Source: TDA 2006b: 8–9.

- building positive relationships by acting as effective mediators between different groups in schools;
- offering a broader enhanced curriculum by running before- and after-school clubs;
- delivering extended services by contributing to the delivery of a range of out-of-school hours learning activities;
- support for school management by taking over some of the administrative and financial tasks from teachers, SENCO, Inclusion Coordinator, Personalised Learning Coordinator or ECM Manager;
- improving the school environment by making it a safe, healthy, pleasant and stimulating place to learn and work in.

The deployment and impact of teaching assistants in schools

The DfES in June 2006, published its research findings on the deployment and impact of support staff in schools. In relation to TAs, the following key findings were noted:

- Teachers have no specifically allocated time to plan and feedback on pupil progress with TAs in mainstream schools;
- The majority of teachers have no formal training to help them work more effectively with support staff in the classroom, however, some are involved in training support staff;

- Much more needs to be done for preparing teachers for working with support staff;
- TAs have a beneficial effect on pupil learning and behaviour and reduce stress levels for teachers;
- TA appraisal is patchy with some schools not undertaking this annual process;
- TAs and welfare staff are most likely to be expected to work extra hours for free;
- The relation between qualifications and wage does not hold for TAs, i.e. those TAs with qualifications above GCSE level are paid the same as those at GCSE level or below;
- The majority of the TA workforce are female;
- Schools with a higher percentage of pupils taking free school meals (FSM), and from ethnic minority groups, had more support staff vacancies, and experienced more recruitment and retention problems;
- Training for support staff is patchy and incidental, with TAs attending mainly school-based INSET or training to deliver national strategy intervention programmes for literacy and numeracy;
- Teachers considered TAs benefited their teaching through: enabling teachers to concentrate on teaching and working with pupils; providing expertise; helping teachers improve the quality of their own teaching; freeing teachers from routine tasks; and, allowing teachers to differentiate work for pupils.

(DfES 2006b: 1–2, Research Brief 776)

Essential factors for the effective deployment of teaching assistants

In 2000 the DfES proposed five essential key elements necessary to support teaching assistants in being effective. These were:

- clear deployment;
- responsibilities explicitly defined;
- an annual review of performance;
- opportunities for ongoing professional development;
- productive partnership working with teachers, other TAs and those from external agencies working directly with children in schools.

The types of teaching assistant support

The TDA in their induction programme for teaching assistants identified four types of support provided by TAs:

- helping with classroom resources and records;
- helping with the care and support of pupils, e.g. escorting pupils to work outside the classroom;
- providing support for learning activities, e.g. supporting teaching and assessment across the curriculum;
- providing support for colleagues, e.g. as members of the school's support staff team they support colleagues by translating school policies into practice and furthering the ethos of the school.

(TDA 2006f: 19)

The three-year school workforce skills strategy to support learning

The School Workforce Development Board (SWDB), in their interim plan *Building the School Team: Our Plans for Support Staff Development 2005–06*, identified the need to develop a framework of skills and competences that would increase the impact of training and development on the day-to-day practice of teaching assistants and other support staff working in schools. The Training and Development Agency for Schools (TDA), in partnership with the SWDB, introduced a three-year national skills strategy 2006–2009, for the wider school workforce to support learning. This strategy is helping to create a coherent training and development system for school support staff, leading to more sustainable workforce improvement in order to meet the educational change agendas such as *Every Child Matters*, extended school services, personalised learning and the 14–19 strategy.

The three-year skills strategy aims to support schools in ensuring that they create a culture where all staff are valued, enjoy high morale and job satisfaction, in order to provide the best possible outcomes for pupils.

The *Every Child Matters* agenda and the extended school services initiative demands that school support staff, and in particular TAs, are sufficiently skilled to work effectively with other professionals, such as health and social care workers.

Every school and every community is unique and different. This requires schools to develop staffing solutions that are appropriate to their phase, type and context, in order to maximise the unique broad range of skills, expertise and talents their staff bring to the learning community.

The three main objectives of the three years skills strategy for the wider school workforce are to:

- Support schools to develop new ways of training and deploying their support staff, i.e. signposting school leaders, TAs and other school support staff to web-based information on training, qualifications and career development; advise school leaders on managing change in the workforce and help them to develop performance management for TAs and other support staff, where it is not already in place.
- Create a framework of standards and qualifications to enable schools to develop the potential of all support staff, i.e. updating existing qualifications, developing new qualifications, reviewing and updating national occupational and professional standards for TAs and HLTAs and other support staff, to reflect the common core of skills and knowledge for those working with children and young people, to ensure closer alignment with the standards for teachers.
- Extend training opportunities to meet the development needs of support staff, e.g. supporting provision for the National Vocational Qualification (NVQ) for TAs at levels 2 and 3; funding and quality assuring the preparation and assessment for HLTA status; developing training for specialist TAs in mathematics and science; and supporting training development in other priority areas to support personalisation of learning, including literacy and numeracy, ICT, behaviour and attendance, SEN, gifted and talented pupils.

The TDA and SWDB have created together the career development framework for school support staff (2006), with guidance materials, which as part of the three-year school workforce skills strategy to support learning, provides schools with information about the training, qualifications and career pathways available to support the new, changing and different roles of TAs and other support staff.

The National Occupational Standards for Teaching Assistants

The National Occupational Standards for Teaching/Classroom Assistants (2001), were considered by the TDA to require updating in view of the changing educational agenda in schools in the twenty-first century. The TDA consulted on the draft version of the revised National Occupational Standards (NOS) for teaching assistants between November 2006 and January 2007. It was recommended that these NOS should be re-titled the National Occupational Standards for Supporting Teaching and Learning in Schools. Supporting teaching and learning may be carried out by TAs within and outside the classroom, or in any setting where teaching and learning takes place, e.g. working off-site on field studies trips and extra-curricular activities such as educational visits; participating in extended school provision and study support. In June 2007, the revised and final version of the NOS for TAs was published.

The revised NOS for TAs incorporate the common core of skills and knowledge for the children's workforce; working with others in a team to progress pupils learning, and appropriate working in multi-disciplinary teams. The common core of skills and knowledge for the children's workforce cover six themes:

- effective communication and engagement with children, young people, parents and carers;
- child and young person development;
- safeguarding and promoting the welfare of the child;
- supporting transitions;
- multi-agency working; and
- sharing information.

The NOS for TAs are statements of competence describing good practice, and are written to measure performance outcomes. They are intended to be used as benchmarks against which to assess the existing levels of skills and knowledge of TAs within the school workforce, and plan the deployment of teaching assistants to build on their individual strengths and expertise.

Using the TA NOS for supporting teaching and learning in schools as the basis of annual TA performance review, allows clear judgements to be made about strengths and current performance, that are consistent with the teaching assistants' job description. They can also be used to identify the development needs and progression opportunities open to TAs.

The revised TA NOS provide clearer progression to higher level teaching assistant (HLTA) status (NVQ Level 4), relevant foundation degrees and qualified teacher status (QTS).

The revised NOS for TAs build on and address gaps in the existing standards for teaching assistants, as well as addressing differences in roles and responsibilities across different educational settings.

The National Vocational Qualifications (NVQ) Structure for TAs, which support the National Occupational Standards for supporting teaching and learning in schools (2007), comprise of 69 units in total. Optional units are grouped under the following five areas A to E:

A Supporting pupils' learning.
B Meeting additional support needs.
C Providing pastoral support.
D Supporting the wider work of the school.
E Working with colleagues.

National Vocational Qualifications (NVQs) for teaching assistants

The revised NVQ for TAs is based on the National Occupational Standards (NOS) for supporting teaching and learning in schools. The NVQ qualifications for TAs are designed to assess how they apply their skills and knowledge to real work practices, using evidence from work situations.

NVQ Level 2 is suitable for TAs new to the role or whose responsibilities are limited in scope. NVQ Level 3 is suitable for experienced TAs whose working role calls for competence across a varied range of responsibilities for supporting teaching and learning in the classroom.

The advantage of the NVQ route is that TAs can work through the qualification at their own pace, studying and undertaking one unit at a time.

TAs require a mentor in school, and to attend external training sessions. An external assessor will pay regular visits to the TA in their school. They will observe the TA at work and look at written evidence to judge achievements against the NOS unit element outcomes. This written evidence can be learning materials the TA has developed or a written statement from a class teacher the TA supports.

TA training and professional development will include blended learning approaches that complement traditional course-based routes of study, for example:

- work shadowing a more experienced TA to observe how they manage aspects of the role;
- on-the-job project work/case study where a TA may shadow a pupil with additional needs to discover how they respond to personalised learning approaches;
- receiving coaching and mentoring from a more experienced TA within their own school or from a neighbouring school;
- visiting other schools to observe relevant aspects of TA working practice;
- e-learning by accessing CD/DVD resources, online learning and email conferencing.

For NVQ Level 2, TAs must pass seven units of competence from the National Occupational Standards for supporting teaching and learning in schools. Five units are mandatory and a further two units must be chosen from a number of options.

TAs do not have to do an NVQ Level 2 before they can study for Level 3, as the point of entry for NVQ study is dependent on the level at which they are working, as well as having the appropriate previous and current experience.

At NVQ Level 3, TAs must pass ten units of competence from the National Occupational Standards for supporting teaching and learning in schools.

Six units are mandatory and a further four optional units must be chosen from Group A to E, of which no more than two units are to be selected from Group E. The optional units studied should be appropriate to the TAs working context, role and responsibilities. Optional units may be selected from within the same group or across different groups. Some credit can be carried forward from NVQ Level 2 to NVQ Level 3.

Table 3.2 provides an overview of the mandatory and optional units for TAs at NVQ Level 2 and Level 3.

Table 3.2 Mandatory and optional units for TAs – NVQ Levels 2 and 3

NVQ level	Mandatory units	Optional units	Group
Level 2	STL1 Provide support for learning activities	STL6 Support literacy and numeracy activities	A
	STL2 Support children's development	STL7 Support the use of ICT for teaching and learning	
	STL3 Help to keep children safe	STL8 Use ICT to support pupils' learning	
	STL4 Contribute to positive relationships	STL9 Observe and report on pupil performance	
	STL5 Provide effective support for your colleagues	STL10 Support children's play and learning	
		STL11 Contribute to supporting bilingual/multilingual pupils	
		STL12 Support a child with disabilities or SEN	
		STL13 Contribute to moving and handling individuals	
		STL14 Support individuals during therapy sessions	
		STL15 Support children and young people's play	
		STL16 Provide displays	D
		STL17 Invigilate tests and exams	D
Level 3	STL3 Help to keep children safe	STL8 Use ICT to support pupils' learning	A
	STL18 Support pupils' learning activities	STL23 Plan, deliver and evaluate teaching and learning activities under the direction of a teacher	A
	STL19 Promote positive behaviour	STL24 Contribute to the planning and evaluation of teaching and learning activities	A
	STL20 Develop and promote positive relationships	STL25 Support literacy development	A
	STL21 Support the development and effectiveness of work teams	STL26 Support numeracy development	A
	STL22 Reflect on and develop practice	STL27 Support implementation of the early years curriculum	A
		STL28 Support teaching and learning in a curriculum area	A
		STL29 Observe and promote pupil performance and development	A
		STL30 Contribute to assessment for learning	A
		STL31 Prepare and maintain the learning environment	A
		STL32 Promote the transfer of learning from outdoor experiences	A
		STL33 Provide literacy and numeracy support to enable pupils to access the wider curriculum	B
		STL34 Support gifted and talented pupils	B
		STL35 Support bilingual/multilingual pupils	B
		STL36 Provide bilingual/multilingual support for teaching and learning	B
		STL37 Contribute to the prevention and management of challenging behaviour in children and young people	B
		STL38 Support children with disabilities or SEN and their families	B

STL39 Support pupils with communication and interaction needs	B
STL40 Support pupils with cognition and learning needs	B
STL41 Support pupils with behaviour, emotional and social development needs	B
STL42 Support pupils with sensory and/or physical impairments	B
STL43 Assist in the administration of medication	B
STL44 Work with children and young people with additional requirements to meet their personal support needs	B
STL45 Promote children's well-being and resilience	C
STL46 Work with young people to safeguard their welfare	C
STL47 Enable young people to be active citizens	C
STL48 Support young people in tackling problems and taking action	C
STL49 Support children and young people during transitions in their lives	C
STL50 Facilitate children and young people's learning and development through mentoring	C
STL51 Contribute to improving attendance	C
STL52 Support children and families through home visiting	C
STL16 Provide displays	D
STL17 Invigilate tests and examinations	D
STL53 Lead an extra-curricular activity	D
STL54 Plan and support self-directed play	D
STL55 Contribute to maintaining pupil records	D
STL56 Monitor and maintain curriculum resources	D
STL57 Organise cover for absent colleagues	D
STL58 Organise and supervise travel	D
STL59 Escort and supervise pupils on educational visits and out-of-school activities	D
STL60 Liaise with parents, carers and families	D
STL61 Provide information to aid policy formation and the improvement of practices and provision	D
STL62 Develop and maintain working relationships with other practitioners	E
STL63 Provide leadership for your team OR	E
STL64 Provide leadership in your area of responsibility	E
STL65 Allocate and check work in your team	E
STL66 Lead and motivate volunteers	E
STL67 Provide learning opportunities for colleagues	E
STL68 Support learning by mentoring in the workplace	E
STL69 Support competence achieved in the workplace	E

Source: TDA 2007.

ECM training and development audit for TAs

The following audit is based on the revised TA National Occupational Standards for supporting teaching and learning in schools, and the revised NVQ structure.

Undertaking the audit will enable TAs to identify aspects of their role which require further professional development in relation to the *Every Child Matters: Change for Children* agenda in schools. Some of the elements on the audit may not be applicable to TAs in respect of their current role and school context they are working in, for example, the elements related to supporting bilingual/multilingual learners where there are no EAL pupils attending, or likely to attend the school in the future.

Table 3.3 ECM training and development audit for teaching assistants

Use the following audit to self-review your ongoing professional development needs for *Every Child Matters*. Not all elements may be appropriate to the TA role.

Indicate your confidence level against each element, using the following rating scale: (1 = emerging and not yet acquired; 2 = developing and in progress; 3 = secure)

A. Supporting teaching and learning	Rating
• Provide support for learning activities	☐
• Support children's developments	☐
• Contribute to positive relationships	☐
• Support literacy and numeracy activities	☐
• Support the use of ICT for teaching and learning	☐
• Use ICT to support pupils' learning	☐
• Observe and report on pupil performance	☐
• Support children's play and learning	☐
• Support children and young people's play	☐
• Support pupils' learning activities	☐
• Develop and promote positive relationships	☐
• Plan, deliver and evaluate teaching and learning activities under the direction of a teacher	☐
• Contribute to the planning and evaluation of teaching and learning activities	☐
• Support literacy development	☐
• Support numeracy development	☐
• Support implementation of the early years curriculum	☐
• Support teaching and learning in a curriculum area	☐
• Observe and promote pupil performance and development	☐
• Contribute to assessment for learning	☐
• Prepare and maintain the learning environment	☐
• Promote the transfer of learning from outdoor experiences	☐
B. Meeting additional support needs	
• Contribute to supporting bilingual/multilingual pupils	☐
• Support a child with disabilities or special educational needs	☐
• Contribute to moving and handling individuals	☐
• Support individuals during therapy sessions	☐
• Promote positive behaviour	☐
• Provide literacy and numeracy support to enable pupils to access wider curriculum	☐
• Support gifted and talented pupils	☐
• Support bilingual/multilingual pupils	☐
• Provide bilingual/multilingual support for teaching and learning	☐
• Contribute to the prevention and management of challenging behaviour in children and young people	☐
• Support children with disabilities or special educational needs	☐
• Support pupils with communication and interaction needs	☐
• Support pupils with cognition and learning needs	☐
• Support pupils with behaviour, emotional and social development needs	☐

Table 3.3 *(Continued)*

• Support pupils with sensory and/or physical needs	☐
• Assist in the administration of medication	☐
• Work with children and young people with additional requirements to meet their personal support needs	☐
C. Providing pastoral support	
• Help to keep children safe	☐
• Promote children's well-being and resilience	☐
• Work with young people to safeguard their welfare	☐
• Enable young people to be active citizens	☐
• Support young people in tackling problems and taking action	☐
• Support children and young people during transitions in their lives	☐
• Facilitate children and young people's learning and development through mentoring	☐
• Contribute to improving attendance	☐
• Support children and families through home visiting	☐
D. Supporting the wider work of the school	
• Provide displays	☐
• Invigilate tests and examinations	☐
• Lead an extra-curricular activity	☐
• Plan and support self-directed play	☐
• Contribute to maintaining pupil records	☐
• Monitor and maintain curriculum resources	☐
• Organise cover for absent colleagues	☐
• Organise and supervise travel	☐
• Escort and supervise pupils on educational trips and out-of-school activities	☐
• Liaise with parents, carers and families	☐
• Provide information to aid policy formation and the improvement of practices and provision	☐
E. Working with colleagues	
• Provide effective support for your colleagues	☐
• Support the development and effectiveness of work teams	☐
• Reflect on and develop practice	☐
• Develop and maintain working relationships with other practitioners	☐
• Provide leadership for your team	☐
• Provide leadership in your area of responsibility	☐
• Allocate and check work in your team	☐
• Lead and motivate volunteers	☐
• Provide learning opportunities for colleagues	☐
• Support learners by mentoring in the workplace	☐
• Support competence achieved in the workplace	☐

Source: based on TDA 2007.

The role of the teaching assistant aligned to the ECM outcomes

The intention of this section of the chapter is to enable TAs to see how the relevant elements of the revised National Occupational Standards for supporting teaching and learning in schools, which informs their job description, aligns with the *Every Child Matters* five outcomes.

A useful initial self-reflection activity for TAs to undertake is to map current role and responsibilities against the five ECM outcomes. Figure 3.1 provides a template to enable TAs to complete this mapping task.

After completing the TA role mapping activity, refer to Table 3.3 which gives examples of TA activities supporting the five ECM outcomes. TAs will be able to see if there are any aspects of

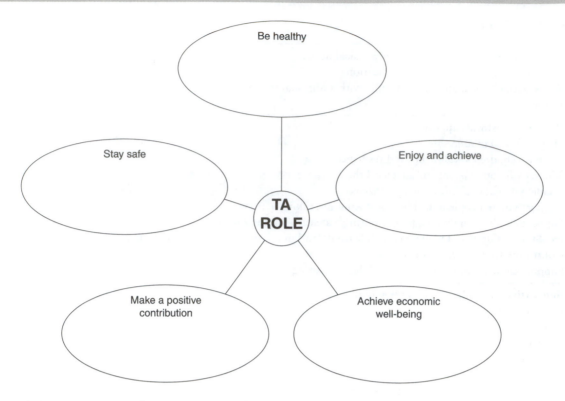

Figure 3.1 Mapping teaching assistant role with the ECM outcomes.

their current and future role, which they need to consider and develop further, in relation to the ECM outcomes. Make a note of these aspects by highlighting them on Table 3.3, and discuss them with your mentor or line manager in school.

Further activities for teaching assistants

The following questions on aspects covered in this chapter are designed to promote further discussion, and help to identify ways forward in enabling TAs to successfully meet their new and changing role in respect of the *Every Child Matters* (ECM) agenda.

- What progress have you already made as a TA in starting to address and respond to the five outcomes of ECM in your daily role?
- What are your personal aims towards meeting the ECM agenda?
- What areas have you identified for further professional development in respect of ECM and the Five Year Strategy for children and learners?
- What barriers, if any, currently prevent you from addressing the ECM outcomes in your support role with pupils?
- What action and next steps do you need to take in order to remove these barriers?
- What would help you to become even more effective in supporting pupils' in achieving the ECM outcomes?
- Who else will you need to work with, both from within and outside school, to help you address the ECM and wider educational change agendas?
- What contributions can you usefully make as a TA to the school's Personalised Learning and ECM Well-being staff team?
- As an experienced TA, what advice would you offer to a newly appointed TA on how to support pupils in successfully achieving the five ECM outcomes?
- How will you ensure you maintain a manageable workload and a healthy work–life balance in view of the competing priorities ECM places on your time?

Table 3.4 Examples of TA activities supporting the five ECM outcomes

Teaching assistants' role in supporting the five *Every Child Matters* outcomes

Be healthy	Stay safe	Enjoy and achieve	Make a positive contribution	Achieve economic well-being
Support teaching and learning in PSHE, and help prepare and develop PSHE materials	Support pupils in utilising ICT, multimedia technology and other equipment safely within the classroom	Support and contribute to the planning of teaching and learning activities under the direction of a teacher	Help pupils with SEN and disabilities, or with sensory and physical impairments to be included and participate in the full range of learning activities	Support pupils to become financially literate
Contribute to and support the Healthy Schools Award	Support pupils in behaving safely and responsibly so as to prevent harm to others and themselves	Support the monitoring and evaluation of pupil outcomes in response to teaching and learning activities	Support pupils with BESD needs to develop positive relationships with others, and to increase their self-confidence	Support pupils to use and apply mathematics
Support and contribute to the management of pupil behaviour by implementing appropriate strategies	Contribute to supporting the safety of pupils with sensory or physical impairments and disabilities in the learning environment	Support pupils' learning activities	Support pupils' rights and choices in learning and play activities	Support and monitor pupils out on work related learning activities or work experience placements
Contribute to supporting pupils with emotional and social development needs to help develop their self-reliance, self-esteem, emotional intelligence and resilience	Contribute to ensuring pupils being supported are safe from bullying, harassment or discrimination	Promote independent learning among pupils supported	Contribute to supporting pupils' communication and intellectual development	Support study support club activities and deliver study support programmes
Contribute to supporting pupils in managing transition and transfer between early years/foundation stage, key stages, and across phases of education	Enable pupils to take safe risks in their learning	Support pupils' learning through the use and application of ICT and other multimedia technology	Support and assist pupils in understanding their communities and their role within them as responsible citizens	
Contribute to establishing, maintaining and ensuring a healthy learning and play environment for pupils	Where appropriate, support the safe moving and handling of pupils with additional needs	Contribute to removing barriers to learning, achievement and participation for a diversity of learners	Support pupil voice by enabling them to communicate their views and interests to others, and to negotiate and influence people and situations	
Support the implementation of the school's health and safety and behaviour policies	Follow the correct procedures for accidents, emergencies, illness and administering medication under supervision	Facilitate pupils learning through modelling examples of good learning, i.e. mentoring pupils how to learn and develop effective learning strategies	Support pupils to tackle problems, make decisions, cope with change, reflect on and learn from their actions	
Contribute to developing and promoting healthy positive productive relationships among pupils, and between pupils and adults	Contribute to the safeguarding of pupils	Support pupils literacy and numeracy development	Help and support pupils to identify how they can transfer learning to other aspects of their lives, as responsible citizens	
	Follow the correct school child protection policy and procedures for reporting any possible child abuse	Support teaching and learning in a curriculum area		

Table 3.4 (*Continued*)

Teaching assistants role in supporting the five *Every Child Matters* outcomes

Be healthy	Stay safe	Enjoy and achieve	Make a positive contribution	Achieve economic well-being
Organise and run a Breakfast club	Follow the correct procedures in the school safety policy	Develop and evaluate materials to support teaching and learning in a curriculum area	Support pupils in developing enterprising behaviour through their involvement in school and community projects, e.g. environmental and business enterprise activities	
Contribute to extended school activities for health and fitness, e.g. sports club	Promote and maintain a safe, secure learning and working environment for pupils	Undertake pre-tutoring with pupils to prepare them for earning in a curriculum area		
	Support pupils' welfare in helping them to assess and manage risk safely	Observe and report on pupil progress, achievements, performance and outcomes in learning and well-being		
	Escort and support the supervision of pupils on educational trips, outings and out-of-school activities	Contribute to pupils' assessment for learning, by supporting them in reviewing their own learning		
		Input pupil data, collect and analyse information on pupil progress, achievements and ECM outcomes to inform future support for learning and well-being		
		Support pupils' continuity and progression in learning at key transition points		
		Help to prepare and maintain the learning environment		
		Prepare learning materials for use with pupils		
		Set up, maintain and dismantle classroom displays		
		Support homework clubs and summer-school activities		
		Support learning activities for gifted and talented pupils		

Table 3.5 Model information leaflet on the role of the teaching assistant

Leafy Lane School The role of the Teaching Assistant in supporting pupils' learning and well-being	Introduction Leafy Lane School recognises the valuable contribution of all teaching assistants (TAs) who are members of the school's Personalised Learning and Well-being Team.

Leafy Lane School
The role of the Teaching Assistant in supporting pupils' learning and well-being

What is the role of the teaching assistant?
TAs work under the direction and guidance of the class teacher.

They act as facilitators, supporters and promoters of pupils' learning and well-being.

The role of the TA in the school has broadened in scope to embrace the *Every Child Matters* and Personalised Learning national initiatives. This entails them in supporting pupils to achieve the five *Every Child Matters* well-being outcomes:

- be healthy;
- stay safe;
- enjoy and achieve;
- make a positive contribution;
- achieve economic well-being.

The role of the TA supporting pupils in the five aspects of personalised learning covers:

- teaching and learning, including the use of ICT;
- assessment for learning;
- curriculum entitlement and choice;
- school organisation for learning;
- beyond the classroom and school.

TAs, along with teachers and other paraprofessionals, contribute first hand evidence to whole school improvement planning and self-evaluation, particularly in relation to judging the quality, effectiveness and impact of additional support and interventions on pupils' achievements, progress and well-being outcomes.

Introduction
Leafy Lane School recognises the valuable contribution of all teaching assistants (TAs) who are members of the school's Personalised Learning and Well-being Team.

The TAs play a crucial role in helping to remove barriers to pupils' learning, along with other members of the team, such as the Learning Mentor, Pupil Counsellor, Family Liaison Worker, and paraprofessionals from external agencies (Health, Social Care and Education), who are working with pupils in school.

The effectiveness of the TAs is dependent on all key stakeholders, e.g. teachers, pupils, parents/carers being clear about the TA's role in promoting inclusion, and supporting pupils personalised learning, personal development and well-being.

This information leaflet is designed to provide a point of reference to all those seeking clarification about the TA's role in Leafy Lane School.

A quick guide to the role of the teaching assistant
Teaching assistants at Leafy Lane School:

- support teaching and learning activities for pupils, under the direction of the class teacher, across the curriculum;
- contribute to the planning and evaluation of teaching and learning activities;
- facilitate pupils' learning and development through mentoring and modelling good learning practices;
- provide targeted literacy and numeracy support to enhance pupils' access to the curriculum;
- maintain a healthy, safe and secure learning environment;
- contribute to the management and promotion of positive pupil behaviour and emotional intelligence;
- provide support to pupils with additional needs, e.g. LDD, SEN, BESD, gifted and talented pupils;
- contribute to assessment for learning by observing, tracking and reporting on pupil progress and performance;
- support and promote pupils' well-being and resilience, helping them to solve problems;
- promote the health and well-being of pupils by helping them to cope with change in their lives, e.g. transition and transfer;
- maintain pupil records of support and intervention;
- escort and supervise pupils on educational trips;
- contribute to the delivery of extended school activities.

Table 3.5 (*continued*)

How do teachers support TAs to be effective?	Which pupils do TAs support and work with?
Teachers can support TAs to be effectively deployed by: • ensuring teacher planning indicates clearly how they will deploy the TA in the lesson to support pupils' learning and well-being; • giving TAs regular feedback on the impact of their support and interventions on pupils' outcomes, achievements and progress; • clarifying shared responsibilities for managing pupils behaviour and well-being; • making the lesson objectives and expected pupil outcomes for learning explicit to the TA; • acknowledging and maximising upon the strengths, expertise and talents of the TA in lessons; • differentiating and adapting the curriculum in partnership with the TA; • modelling good learning and assessment for learning approaches to TAs to use with pupils being supported; • guiding TAs on using effective open questioning and thinking skills with pupils during their support work; • enabling them to utilise multimedia technology and ICT to support and enhance pupils learning.	Teaching assistants target and tailor their support for different groups of pupils identified as having additional needs who may be underachieving, e.g. girls or boys; those at risk of being excluded or disaffected; those who are poor attenders; those from ethnic minority and faith groups, Travellers, asylum seekers and refugees; those learning English as an additional language (EAL); young carers; those with LDD, SEN; sick children; those from families under stress; pregnant school girls and teenage mothers; children in public care 'looked after' by the local authority; gifted and talented pupils; drug dependent young people; those experiencing mental health problems, and those experiencing significant challenging behaviour. **How is TA support allocated?** The nature and level of TA support pupils receive is allocated according to identified needs arising from the outcome of the Common Assessment Framework review process, or the provision specified on a pupil's statement of special educational needs. TA support is also allotted as an outcome of the annual review of the whole school inclusion provision map. This entails judging the effectiveness of additional interventions on improving pupils' progress in learning, their personal development and well-being.

POST TITLE:	Teaching Assistant for Personalised Learning and Well-being
GRADE:	(Level 1, 2 or 3)
PAY SCALE:	SCP 4–11, or SCP 12–17, or SCP 18–25
HOURS OF WORK:	28 hours per week pro rata
PLACE OF EMPLOYMENT:	Leafy Lane Community School
RESPONSIBLE TO:	The Every Child Matters Manager or Director
LIAISES WITH:	Class/Subject teachers, Leading Teachers, INCO, SENCO, Personalised Learning Coordinator, Extended School Coordinator, practitioners from external agencies
MAIN PURPOSE:	As a valued member of the school's Personalised Learning and ECM Well-being team to work with individual and groups of pupils under the direction of the teacher, to provide tailored support for teaching, personalised learning and well-being, in order to deliver the *Every Child Matters* (ECM) outcomes.

MAIN DUTIES

Supporting pupils' personalised learning

- Support pupils' learning activities across the cirriculum, tailoring support strategies to match learners' needs
- Support pupils to become independent and collaborative learners
- Support pupils' learning through the use of ICT and multimedia technology
- Utilise accelerated learning approaches to support pupils' learning
- Observe, feedback and report on pupil performance and achievements
- Promote pupils' assessment for learning by supporting them to review their own learning and progress
- Promote and support inclusion by removing barriers to learning and participation
- Prepare learning materials

- Support the development and maintenance of a healthy, safe and secure learning environment
- Contribute to the planning, delivery and evaluation of teaching activities
- Support teaching in a specific curriculum area
- Prepare and maintain the learning environment
- Support, and prepare for, the use of ICT in the classroom
- Support teaching and learning in a curriculum subject area
- Prepare, maintain and use equipment and subject specific resources to improve pupils' curriculum access
- Develop and evaluate materials to support teaching and learning in a curriculum area
- Contribute to the monitoring and assessment of pupils progress in a curriculum area

Meeting additional support needs

- Provide support to pupils with additional needs, which includes gifted and talented pupils as well as those with learning difficulties and disabilities
- Contribute to the management of pupils' behaviour, supporting them to take responsibility for their own behaviour

- Provide support for literacy and numeracy to enhance wider curriculum access
- Support the delivery of targeted interventions and programmes for literacy and numeracy, feeding back to teachers on the impact on pupils' progress and ECM outcomes

Providing pastoral support for pupil well-being

- Act as a learning guide or life coach to targeted vulnerable pupils
- Promote and support pupils' well-being and resilience, helping them to form positive and productive relationships with others

- Promote and support the development of pupils' emotional intelligence
- Support pupils to cope with change during transfer and transition

Supporting the wider work of the school

- Comply with school policies and procedures related to child protection, safeguarding children, health and safety, confidentiality and data protection, *Every Child Matters*, equal opportunities and inclusion
- Escort and supervise pupils on educational visits and out-of-school activities, where appropriate
- Contribute pupil information to the CAF process
- Support teachers in the administration of tests and examinations

- Contribute to maintaining pupils' records
- Provide clerical/administrative support to teachers, e.g. photocopying, typing, filing, collecting money
- Contribute to the school's self-evaluation and school improvement planning processes
- Contribute to supporting pupils in extended school learning activities
- Assist with the display of learners' work and achievements

Working with colleagues, including supporting the school's personalised learning and ECM well-being team

- Mediate between pupils, teachers and other professionals to support and develop pupils' learning and well-being
- Support and maintain productive, collaborative partnership working relationships with other front-line workers from external agencies, and colleagues
- Support and contribute to the development and effectiveness of teamwork

- Provide effective support for other colleagues
- Take an active part in developing your own continuing professional development, maintaining a portfolio of evidence to support your annual formal appraisal review
- Undertake other duties commensurate with the post, as allocated by the headteacher

Figure 3.2 Model TA job description. Source: based on TDA 2007.

4

Teaching Assistants Supporting Learners to be Healthy and Stay Safe

Introduction

The first part of the chapter clarifies what is meant by being healthy. It goes on to describe why the good health of learners is important in removing barriers to achievement. It refers the reader to the relevance of the National Healthy Schools Standard (NHSS), the Personal, Social and Health Education (PSHE) programme, the Social and Emotional Aspects of Learning (SEAL) and the Social, Emotional and Behavioural Skills (SEBS) strategies in supporting and developing learners' health and well-being, which in turn helps to promote and enhance learning. Practical suggestions are offered as to how TAs can utilise existing strategies to support learners' health and well-being, while acknowledging the valuable contributions TAs already make, in complementing the work of other health care professionals in schools. The second part of the chapter focuses on the concept and importance of learners staying safe. It emphasises TAs' contributions to safeguarding the welfare of learners, and the importance of following the correct child protection procedures in schools. The chapter concludes with familiar practical strategies and approaches TAs can utilise in supporting and promoting the safety and welfare of learners.

Being healthy

Every Child Matters (DfES 2003) commented that children cannot learn effectively if health problems create barriers. The government's intention for all schools to become healthy schools by 2009, recognises the importance of investing in good physical, emotional and mental health to assist in promoting social inclusion, developing healthy behaviours, improving attendance, enhancing teaching and learning, raising levels of pupils' achievement and improving educational standards overall. A healthy school provides accessible and relevant information to enable pupils to make informed decisions and choices about their health and pursuing a healthy lifestyle. It also recognises the need to provide a physical and social environment that is conducive to learning.

National initiatives and strategies

TAs are already supporting the delivery of the Social and Emotional Aspects of Learning (SEAL) and Silver SEAL whole school intervention programmes as part of the primary national strategy. They are also supporting the delivery of the Social, Emotional and Behavioural Skills (SEBS) programme as part of the secondary national strategy, both of which contribute significantly to the *Every Child Matters* (ECM) outcome of being healthy, and which promote resilience, positive behaviour and effective learning. SEAL and SEBS cover self-awareness, managing feelings, motivation, empathy and social skills. TAs will be supporting learners in schools that are either working towards achieving national Healthy School status, or in those that have already achieved this recognition. In either case, schools will be meeting specific health criteria related to four themes:

- PSHE (including sex and relationship education and drug education);
- healthy eating;
- physical activity;
- emotional health and well-being (EHWB), including bullying.

Promoting emotional health and well-being (EHWB) through the National Healthy School Standard (NHSS) brings valuable benefits to schools because it:

- helps to develop a healthy, successful, inclusive school community;
- helps pupils and staff feel happier and more motivated, and helps to reduce mental health problems;
- openly addresses issues by enabling pupils to understand what they are feeling and building their confidence to learn;
- identifies and supports the emotional health needs of staff;
- helps to develop pupils' social, emotional and behavioural skills;
- helps to reduce bullying.

Emotional well-being

Emotional well-being refers to the holistic, subjective state which is present when a range of feelings such as energy, confidence, self-awareness, openness, enjoyment, happiness, calm, empathy and caring are combined, well-managed and balanced. Emotional well-being is also referred to as emotional literacy, emotional intelligence and social and emotional competence. Schools have a direct influence on the emotional health of learners and staff, which in turn has an impact on academic and other achievement.

Emotional health and well-being (EHWB) forms part of the wider concept of promoting positive mental health and addressing mental health difficulties. TAs, along with other front-line workers from external agencies can help pupils to recognise, respond to and manage their emotions through approaches such as circle time, restorative justice, anger management and conflict resolution. Positive EHWB contributes to better behaviour, attendance and engagement in the learning process among learners.

Children and young people in schools consider having people to talk to (peers and trusting adults), achieving personally, being praised and feeling positive about oneself have the greatest impact on their emotional well-being.

The factors that make pupils feel stressed and which are detrimental to their emotional well-being are conflict, confrontation with authority, restriction of autonomy, which includes pupil voice, and exclusion and isolation by peers.

Social, Emotional and Behavioural Skills (SEBS)

TAs need to be aware of the range of SEBS that contribute to learners' emotional health and well-being. These include:

- being an effective and successful learner;
- making and sustaining friendships;
- dealing with and resolving conflict effectively and fairly;
- being able to solve problems with others and alone;
- managing strong feelings such as frustration, anger and anxiety;
- recovering from setbacks and persisting in the face of difficulties;
- working and playing cooperatively;
- competing fairly and losing with dignity and respect for competitors;
- recognising and standing up for your rights and the rights of others;
- understanding and valuing the differences between people and respecting the right of others to have different beliefs and values.

The link between emotional health, well-being and learning

On 14 February 2007, UNICEF published a report entitled: *Child Poverty: An Overview of Child Well-being in Rich Countries*. Out of 21 industrialised countries the best place for children and young people's well-being was the Netherlands, and the worst place was the UK. Although the UK ranked higher in educational well-being, it lagged behind other countries in relative poverty and deprivation; quality of children's relationships with their parents and peers; child health and safety; behaviour and risk-taking; and children's subjective sense of well-being.

The development of emotional health and well-being, along with the basic needs of safety, belonging and self-esteem, help pupils to achieve their potential and learn more effectively. Positive relationships at home and in school enable the child and young person to build their self-esteem and resilience, and to know how to relate to and behave with others.

Definition of resilience

Resilience as a process is defined as the positive adaptation, 'bouncing back', coping, recovering in the face of severe adversities. Resilient children and young people are those who resist adversity, manage to cope with uncertainty in challenging or threatening circumstances, and who recover successfully from trauma.

Factors that help build resilience

The factors that help to build resilience in children and young people include:

- a secure base where the child feels a sense of belonging and security, e.g. a safe, happy home; a nurturing environment at home and school;
- good self-esteem – a good sense of worth and competence;
- self-efficacy – a sense of mastery and control, an accurate understanding of personal strengths and limitations, i.e. a belief that one's efforts can make a difference;
- one secure attachment relationship with an unconditionally supportive adult, e.g. parent/carer;

- a committed mentor, life coach or learning guide who acts as a positive adult role model;
- access to wider supports such as extended family and friends;
- positive nursery, school and/or community experiences;
- participation in a range of extra-curricular activities;
- the capacity to re-frame adversities in order that the beneficial, as well as the damaging effects, are recognised;
- not to be excessively sheltered from challenging situations that provide opportunities to develop coping skills;
- the ability/opportunity to help others and to make a difference through part-time work, volunteering.

Where a child or young person experiences and witnesses unpredictable, frightening or abusive interactions on a regular basis at home, this can affect their ability to form trusting relationships with peers and adults in school, thus inhibiting their emotional well-being, as well as their learning.

Abraham Maslow's hierarchy of needs underpins the *Every Child Matters* five outcomes for children and young people, particularly in relation to adopting a holistic approach to recognising the basic needs (levels 1, 2 and 3) and higher order needs (levels 4 and 5), of the individual.

Table 4.1 provides a useful overview for TAs in identifying the everyday support activities that will enhance learners' health and well-being in school.

Facts about children and young people's well-being

When TAs are supporting the emotional well-being of children and young people, they need to be aware that:

- Social and emotional skills and attainment are mutually reinforcing, for example, negative emotions like sadness or anger can create a barrier to learning, while positive feelings help to promote learning.
- When emotional well-being deteriorates the result is often the onset of mental health problems, ranging from depression, anxiety and anorexia to violent delinquency.
- There has been a 100 per cent increase since the early 1990s in the prevalence of emotional problems and conduct disorders among young people, as a result of family breakdown, junk food diets, binge-drinking, drug abuse, exam pressure, and media images of super models and celebrity lifestyles.
- One in ten children and young people aged 5–16 in Great Britain have a clinically recognisable mental health disorder, that is a total of 1.1 million children.
- There is a strong link between mental and emotional health and rates of smoking, drinking and cannabis use among children aged 11–15, for example, over 40 per cent who smoked regularly, almost a quarter of those who drank regularly, and almost half of those who took cannabis at least once a month had an emotional or mental disorder.
- A third of teenagers aged 14–16 with conduct disorders characterised by aggressive, disruptive or anti-social behaviour drink alcohol at least once a week.
- Over two-fifths (44 per cent) of children with an emotional disorder are behind in their intellectual development, with 23 per cent being two or more years behind, compared with 24 per cent and 9 per cent of other children.

(NCH 2007a: 1–3)

Table 4.1 Maslow's hierarchy of needs and health and well-being in schools

Maslow's range of needs	Desirable experiences for children and young people	Nature of support and provision in school
1 Physiological or survival needs	• Warmth • Food • Shelter • Seeing, hearing and taking part in what's going on • Safe physical exploration • Getting to know your own body and its strengths and limits	• Comfortable classroom/learning environment with well-positioned equipment • Healthy meals and snacks; access to drinking water when needed • Breakfast club • Indoor and outdoor play areas • Sensory trails • Sport and challenge activities • Ponds and natural or wild areas
2 Safety needs	• Having boundaries • Having basic needs met • Knowing you are in safe hands	• Secure, risk-assessed sites • Consistent, caring supervision • Simple, clearly explained rules • Clear policies and procedures for tackling and minimising bullying
3 Love, affection and belonging	• Feeling cared for • Having others look out for you when you can't do it for yourself • Having responsibilities and opportunities to effect change • Recognising feeling states in yourself and others • Talking, listening, exploring and reflecting on experiences	• Positive relationships and interactions with staff and peers • Diversity and difference is valued and celebrated • Places, times and people you can go to for help and support • Pupil involvement in setting rules and expectations • Work displayed on the wall • Coat pegs with individual names on • Opportunities for group work • Peer support programmes
4 Self-esteem	• Being valued, accepted and celebrated • Being noticed and listened to • Influencing outcomes • Being supported to take responsibility for outcomes with increasing independence	• 'Star of the day'; events to be the focus of positive attention • Use of praise • Use of appropriate language to correct behaviour • Rewards and recognition systems • Opportunities to have special responsibilities
5 Self-actualisation (fulfilment)	• Exploring ideas and learning new things • Being creative • Developing talents and stretching yourself • Having an internal structure of values and principles • Recognising and using signs, symbols, image and metaphor • Being reflective • Developing shared meanings and a shared narrative (ways of talking about what happens)	• Lessons which provide stimulation, challenge and opportunities to use diverse talents • Values and rights education • Taught courses for SEBS, including thinking and problem-solving skills • Time for reflection • Use of storytelling, language, literature and metaphor in the curriculum • Drama, art, music and movement that communicates feelings, meanings, experiences • Positive modelling by all school staff

Source: DH/DfES 2004: 4.

Practical strategies for TAs supporting learners' physical, emotional health and well-being

- TAs supporting breakfast clubs follow the school's healthy food policy by offering pupils healthier food and drink options.
- TAs overseeing snack time ensure learners eat and drink in a calm, clean and welcoming environment, where pupils have the opportunity to utilise social interaction skills and practice table manners.
- Where TAs may undertake lunchtime supervision, to support and monitor learners' healthy food and drink choices, encouraging them to avoid fizzy drinks high in sugar, and foods high in sugar, fat and salt.
- TAs ensure that pupils being supported have access to drinking water throughout the school day.
- TAs contribute to extended school activities which offer learners opportunities to develop physical fitness and well-being, e.g. dance club, keep-fit class.
- TAs support the school's travel plan and set an example to learners' healthy lifestyles by walking or cycling to school, walking the 'Playground Mile' with pupils, and/or organising the school's 'Walking Bus' scheme.
- TAs may support pupil participation in School Council or Focus Group discussions relating to health, behaviour, PSHE and well-being issues.
- TAs ensure that they provide an emotionally intelligent learning support environment which is calm, blame free, respectful and welcoming.
- TAs and teachers ensure that learners' work is displayed attractively and that pupils have a say in what work is displayed, and where.
- TAs support pupils to gain the maximum benefit from Circle Time, where learners can explore and share their feelings with others, understand how to manage their emotions, how to make wise behaviour choices, respect others and respond appropriately in situations.
- TAs as active listeners and trusting adults, respect confidentiality, and refer learners to appropriate pastoral and professional support, to enable them to cope with, for example, bereavement, mental health difficulties or bullying.
- TAs adopt active listening skills with learners who have concerns and use positive language rather than negative terms such as 'but', for example, the TA dialogue with a troubled pupil may take the following form: *'Can you tell me about your concern and what is troubling you? … From what you have told me I can understand why you may feel like that, and I realise it must be hard for you and that you have tried your best, however, have you thought about trying this approach next time you meet that situation again.'*
- TAs during support and interventions promote learners' spiritual, moral, social and cultural development.
- TAs, in partnership with the Learning Mentor, train pupils to become pupil buddies and befrienders to isolated peers.
- TAs consistently reinforce the school's behaviour policy and classroom routines, for example the four 'R's: ensure pupils' rights to learn are respected; that learners are given responsibility for making positive behaviour choices and TAs phrase behaviour requests positively; TAs reinforce classroom rules, i.e. no put-downs, no name calling, no interfering with others work or belongings, and no swearing; and, reinforce routines in relation to classroom conduct, e.g. protocols for entering and exiting the classroom, asking and answering questions, moving around the classroom.

- TAs encourage learners being supported to utilise positive self-talk.
- TAs utilise role play, scenarios and social stories to help learners to understand and interpret social interactions with others appropriately and to know how to react and behave in similar situations.
- TAs help to minimise learners impulsive behaviour by encouraging them to stop and listen; look at the TA/teacher and think about their actions; answer positively and respond appropriately.
- TAs to encourage learners to practice social, emotional and behavioural management skills learnt at school in different contexts, e.g. at home, when out with friends in the community.
- TAs support pupils to manage their anger by utilising strategies such as deep breathing, counting to ten under their breath, thinking positively about something else more pleasant, using a stress ball, taking time out and cooling off.
- TAs ensure that they give instant feedback when learners being supported react and behave in an appropriate way, without over-using praise excessively. Positive affirmations and appropriate rewards are used to acknowledge progress in EHWB, e.g. *'I liked it when you...'*.

Table 4.2 provides TAs with a guide to what are acceptable and unacceptable levels of behaviour from the learners they support within and beyond the classroom, based on the latest Ofsted guidance.

Table 4.2 Evaluating learners' behaviour

Ofsted grade	Behaviour descriptor
Outstanding (1)	Learners' mature, thoughtful behaviour is an outstanding factor in their successful learning and creates an extremely positive school ethos. Learners are very supportive of each other in lessons and show great consideration of each other's interests around the school.
Good (2)	Learners' behaviour makes a strong contribution to good learning in lessons. Their behaviour is welcoming and positive. They show responsibility in responding to routine expectations, set consistent standards for themselves and need only rare guidance from staff about how to conduct themselves. They behave well towards each other, showing respect and encourage others to conduct themselves equally well.
Satisfactory (3)	Learners' behaviour is acceptable in the classroom so that it does not interfere with learning and time is not wasted. They can work on their own or in small groups. Around the school, learners' behaviour is secure and well-ordered so that public spaces are normally safe and calm. Learners themselves feel secure and understand how to deal with bullying or other problems. Learners generally respond appropriately to sanctions.
Inadequate (4)	Learners' behaviour inhibits their progress or well-being in lessons more often than a few isolated occasions. Time may be wasted through persistent low-level disruption or occasional deliberate disobedience, for example by interfering with others' concentration during independent work. It may also be reflected in lateness and a lack of attention such as extensive off-task chatter. Some learners show a lack of respect for – or direct challenge to – adults or other young people, including instances of racism, sexism and other forms of bullying.

Source: Ofsted 2007c: 10.

Staying safe

Every Child Matters (DfES 2003) commented that children and young people cannot learn effectively if they do not feel safe. The ECM outcome staying safe refers to children and young people being safe from maltreatment, neglect, violence and sexual exploitation; safe from accidental injury and death; safe from bullying and discrimination; safe from crime and anti-social behaviour; have security and stability in their lives and are cared for.

Safeguarding the welfare of children and young people

TAs, like all other staff working in schools, have a duty to safeguard and promote the welfare of learners. This means taking reasonable measures and appropriate action to ensure that children and young people's welfare does not suffer as a result of risks of harm.

Safeguarding covers issues such as health, safety and bullying; arrangements for meeting the medical needs of children with medical conditions; providing first aid; school security and safety on educational visits; safeguarding against drugs and substance misuse.

Child protection relates to where a child or young person is suffering or is likely to suffer significant harm such as ill treatment or the impairment of health and development, including impairment suffered from seeing or hearing the ill treatment of others. Ill treatment includes sexual abuse, and emotional ill treatment such as conveying to children and young people that they are worthless, unloved or inadequate.

Domestic violence and abuse can affect children and young people's emotional and physical safety and welfare. The child or young person may feel guilty because they think the abuse is their fault. TAs need to look out for the effects of this, particularly among the vulnerable learners they support. There may be unexplained absences from school, as the child or young person stays home to support their mother who is being abused. The child or young person may attend school even when they are ill, because they don't feel safe at home. Unfinished homework due to domestic turmoil occurring may become an issue. Learners feel tired and are unable to concentrate, as a result of not sleeping or experiencing anxiety. Extremes of behaviour may be present, for example being quiet and withdrawn or disruptive and angry. Eating disorders may also be present, e.g. anorexia or over-eating. Children and young people who witness and live with abuse and violence may miss out on social support from peers, as they feel unable to invite friends back to their house.

TAs should refer any concerns related to safeguarding or child protection to the designated senior member of staff in school with responsibility for child protection. TAs will follow consistently the school's child protection and safeguarding policies and procedures, and keep child protection training up-to-date every three years.

In the instances where a learner during support discloses to the TA that they are experiencing abuse, or reveals information that raises serious concerns, then the TA must inform and refer the exact cause for concern or disclosure to the senior member of staff taking the lead role for child protection, during the same working day. The TA is entitled to know the outcome of the referral. When a pupil makes a disclosure, the TA must be careful not to ask the child or young person any leading questions when ascertaining basic facts. TAs must exercise care and sensitivity when sharing information, in order to respect confidentiality, without compromising the safety of the child or young person.

Further information about safeguarding the welfare of learners is at:

www.everychildmatters.gov.uk/search/?asset=dowmeat&id=17378

Bullying

One in four pupils report that they are bullied in school, with 31 per cent of children experiencing bullying during childhood. The government defines bullying as repetitive, wilful or persistent behaviour that is intended to cause harm, and leave the pupil being bullied feeling defenceless. Bullying, whether physical or emotional, can have a negative impact on a learners' emotional safety, health and well-being. Bullying includes: name-calling, taunting, mocking, making offensive comments, kicking, hitting, pushing, taking belongings, gossiping, excluding people from groups, spreading hurtful and untruthful rumours, inappropriate text messaging and emailing, sending offensive or degrading images by phone or via the Internet (cyberbullying).

What is cyberbullying?

Cyberbullying is when an individual is tormented, threatened, harassed, humiliated or embarrassed by another individual or group repeatedly over time, using the Internet, interactive and digital technologies or mobile phones. Unfortunately, cyberbullying can occur outside school hours as well as in school time, and is done generally by children and young people in the same class or year group.

Today's children and young people are highly technologically literate. Of those aged 8–15, 64 per cent have access to the Internet at home, and 65 per cent have their own mobile phone, making virtual communication difficult for adults to mediate.

Types of cyberbullying

There are seven different types of cyberbullying.

- Text message bullying – when unwelcome threatening texts are sent and received.
- Picture/video-clip bullying via mobile phone cameras – where unpleasant images are sent to others, e.g. 'happy slapping'.
- Phone call bullying via mobile phone – silent calls or abusive messages being sent to harass others.
- Email bullying – messages sent to bully or threaten others using a pseudonym, anonymously or in someone else's name.
- Chatroom bullying – menacing or upsetting responses sent to children and young people when they are accessing a web-based chatroom.
- Bullying through instant messaging (IM) – Internet-based bullying where children and young people receive unpleasant messages directly when they are conducting real-time online conversations.
- Bullying via website – includes the use of defamatory blogs (web logs), personal websites, online personal polling sites and social networking sites.

Facts and figures about cyberbullying

Research commissioned by the Anti-Bullying Alliance in 2005, and the NCH/Tesco Mobile survey, 2005 found that:

- Between one-fifth and one-quarter of children and young people have been cyberbullied at least once over the previous few months.
- Phone calls, text messages and email were the most common.
- More cyberbullying takes place outside school than in school.
- Girls are more likely than boys to be involved in cyberbullying in school, usually by phone.
- Boys are more likely to be involved in text messaging, followed by picture/video clip or website bullying.
- Picture/video clip and phone call bullying were perceived as most harmful.
- Website and text bullying were equated in impact to other forms of bullying.
- Around one-third of those being cyberbullied told no one about the bullying.
- One-quarter of young people who had been cyberbullied said that knowing how to get hold of and speak to an expert at dealing with cyberbullying would have made a difference.
- 15 per cent of young people indicated that knowing there was a staff member at school dedicated to stopping cyberbullying was a help.
- 13 per cent said that knowing of a website with advice and tips would have helped them.
- One-fifth of parents think that mobile bullying is not common or never happens.

Practical strategies for TAs to prevent cyberbullying

TAs through their direct support for pupils' learning, and in particular working with pupils using ICT and other interactive and digital technologies, are well placed to guide pupils in the safe use of technology and mobile phones. Pupils may also choose to inform a TA if they are being cyberbullied. Listed below are some practical approaches and guidance for TAs to prevent cyberbullying between pupils.

- Be familiar with, and apply the school policy, in monitoring electronic messages and images when pupils are using ICT.
- Make pupils aware of personal privacy rights, and safety in using and accessing photographic images and material posted on any electronic platform.
- Ensure learners fully understand the value of e-communication and the risks and consequences of their actions if they misuse the Internet or mobile phone, i.e. lose their Internet Service Provider (ISP) or instant messaging (IM) accounts.
- Where a pupil reports cyberbullying to you, refer this to a senior member of staff in school, and encourage the young person not to reply to any electronic messages or calls, but to retain the evidence.
- Ensure pupils know how to use voicemail to vet any incoming mobile phone calls, and don't open any files or accept, or respond to emails from unknown sources.
- Ensure the pupil informs their parents about any cyberbullying and ask them to contact the ISP about the problem and, where necessary, change their phone number.
- Provide pupils with some quick-fix solutions in dealing with cyberbullying, e.g. hang up the phone, don't give name or number to any unknown caller, close down computer, take deep breaths, think about or do something else, talk to a friend or adult about the incident(s).
- Give pupils a copy of the NCH 'Top 10 tips' poster on text bullying.

Further information about cyberbullying and how to prevent it can be found on the following websites:

www.kidscape.org.uk
www.wiredsafety.org

www.stoptextbully.com
www.bullybeware.com
www.nch.org.uk
www.beyondbullying.com/teachers/4292.html

Children and young people who are the victims of bullying experience unhappiness, low self-esteem, anxiety, depression, withdrawal, self-harm or suicide. They live in constant fear of being bullied, whether at school or at home, and therefore feel unsafe, and unable to concentrate on school work or enjoy their learning.

Every Child Matters highlights the damage that bullying can do to children and young people's educational and social achievements. Staff in schools, including TAs, need to focus on tackling and changing the behaviour of the pupils doing the bullying. Some TAs may already contribute to supporting pupils who are either victims or perpetrators of bullying in schools, as part of Behaviour Improvement Programmes (BIP). They will be ensuring that their support and interventions to address and improve any bullying issues among learners follow the school's anti-bullying policy.

TAs reinforce positive behaviour to the learners they work with by modelling tolerance, respect, empathy and self-awareness, which helps to build up pupils' understanding and resilience, social responsibility and counteracts bullying.

Practical anti-bullying strategies for TAs supporting pupils

Ofsted (2003), in their report on bullying, identified the following features of effective practice to overcome bullying.

- Promoting a strong ethos of tolerance and respect.
- Zero tolerance of bullying with speedy interventions and support to address the issue.
- Supporting the victims of bullying to be more assertive and the perpetrators of bullying to develop emotional intelligence, learning how to be emphatic and socially responsible.
- Act as a champion for learners in relation to actively listening to any concerns or worries they may share relating to safety.
- Making yourself approachable and available to pupils who may be being intimidated by other learners and enabling them to access a quiet room or safe haven during break and lunchtimes.
- Coach older pupils to become 'buddies' and befrienders to younger pupils, and to participate together in extended school activities.
- Support and promote 'circle of friends' and peer mediation approaches with learners who are being bullied, or who are bullying others.
- Follow-up provided for bullies and those who have experienced being bullied, to monitor pupils' welfare and safety.

Further information about preventing bullying can be found at:

www.dfes.gov.uk/bullying
www.antibullying.net
www.bullying.co.uk

Mediation

TAs acting as mediators can contribute significantly to settling disputes between pupils by creating favourable conditions. This will include:

- providing an appropriate environment such as a neutral venue with appropriate seating arrangements and security away from the place of conflict and dispute;
- establishing basic ground rules which help to explain the process of mediation to the parties in dispute;
- helping to reduce anxiety, aggression, intimidation and pressure by providing an emotionally intelligent environment;
- interpreting the non-verbal behaviour of participants accurately as well as being an active listener and observer;
- being solution focused in resolving disputes between pupils, acting as catalysts for creative problem solving, and brainstorming with the pupils concerned to reach consensual settlement options;
- adopting restorative justice approaches to resolve conflict, restore relationships, develop empathy, rapport and appropriate behaviour management among pupils in dispute with each other, through building mutual respect by utilising circle time, circle of friends, School Council, peer mediation.

Table 4.3 provides an overview of changing perspectives about restorative justice.

Staying safe – TAs supporting pupils with medical needs

'Medical needs' covers those pupils who have longer term significant and chronic medical conditions such as epilepsy, cystic fibrosis, asthma, diabetes, or who have allergic reactions (anaphylaxis) as a result of exposure to certain foods such as nuts, dairy produce or the venom of stinging insects.

TAs may be assigned to support learners with medical needs, and supervise them undertaking some activities in lessons such as PE or Design and Technology where the safe use of equipment is necessary.

The learner with medical needs' healthcare plan will identify the necessary safety measures required to ensure they or their peers are not put at risk. The school will make reasonable adjustments under the Disability Discrimination Act (DDA) 1995, to ensure that those pupils with medical needs have access to the curriculum, extended school activities and all aspects of school life, including participating in school trips; the provision of written materials in alternative formats, where necessary; and access to school premises and facilities.

TAs, along with the teaching staff, will need to be provided with advice on the specific health issues and medical needs of the pupils they work with from school health service professionals, i.e. school doctor, school nurse, health visitor, as well as parents/carers of the child or young person.

While there is no legal duty that requires school staff to administer medicines to pupils with medical needs, some TAs may have the administration of medicines and the personal care of such pupils included in their contract of employment and in their job description, as a core role. Where this is the case, it is essential that the TA is appropriately guided and trained by health professionals, to manage medicines and carry out personal care, as part of their duties.

Table 4.3 Restorative justice in the school context

Old perspective about retributive justice	New restorative justice perspective
Wrongdoing or misdemeanour is defined as breaking the school rules and/or letting the school down	Wrongdoing or misdemeanour is defined as adversely affecting others due to harm being done to the well-being of one person or a group
Focus on establishing blame or guilt on the past; what happened? who did it?	Focus on problem solving by expressing feelings and needs and exploring how to meet them in the future
Adversarial relationship and process – wrongdoer in conflict with a person in authority, who decides on the punishment or penalty	Dialogue and negotiation – everyone involved in communicating and cooperating with each other
Imposition of unpleasantness or pain to punish and deter/prevent	Restitution as a means of restoring both or all parties, with the goal being reconciliation and future responsibility
Attention to the right rules and adherence to the correct process	Attention being given to forming the right relationships and achievement of the desired outcome
Wrongdoing represented as the individual versus the school (impersonal and abstract)	Wrongdoing and misdemeanour conflicts with opportunities for learning
One social injury replaced by another	Focus on repair of social injury or damage
School community as spectators, represented by a staff member dealing with the situation	School community involved in facilitating restoration
Pupils affected by wrongdoing or misdemeanour not necessarily involved; victims' needs are often ignored; and, they can feel powerless. Matter dealt with by those in authority	Encouragement of all concerned to be involved – empowerment
Wrongdoer accountability defined in terms of receiving punishment	Wrongdoer accountability defined as understanding the impact of one's actions, taking responsibility, seeing it as a consequence of choices and helping to decide how to put things right

Source: Hopkins 1999: 2–3 and 21–22.

A risk assessment to the health and safety of staff, pupils and others will be essential, with appropriate measures put in place to manage any identified risks. TAs, like any other staff, will follow the procedures set out in the school's health and safety policy, which incorporates managing the administration of medicines, and supporting pupils with complex health needs. TAs supporting pupils with medical needs should be aware of the possible side effects of the medication taken, which may create barriers to learning, and know what to do if they occur.

Where a TA is designated to administer and supervise pupils taking medication, it is important in the interests of health and safety that:

- the medicine should be in the original container as dispensed by a pharmacist, which includes the prescriber's instructions for administration, the child's name and the expiry date of the medication;
- the dose on the label of the container from the pharmacist must be adhered to, and a careful record kept when medication has been administered, who by, and who to, as a duty to care;
- controlled drugs and medicines should be locked in a non-portable container in school, or refrigerated where indicated, and a careful record of the medicines stored should be made;
- where rectal medication is administered to a pupil, this should be witnessed by a second adult in school;
- when the controlled drug or prescription medicine is no longer required by the pupil in school, any surplus or unwanted medicines and drugs should be returned to the parents/carers to take back to the dispensing pharmacist at the chemist;
- a member of staff should never give a non-prescribed medicine to a pupil unless prior written permission from the parents/carers has been secured;
- any pupil under 16 should never be given aspirin or medicines containing ibuprofen unless prescribed by a doctor;
- in the instance where a pupil refuses to take their medication, the TA or member of staff concerned should inform the parents/carers of this on the day, and make a record of the refusal. The TA/staff member should not force the pupil to take the medication if they refuse;
- the side effects of controlled drugs and medicines taken by pupils should be known as these may affect their learning capacity or physical abilities, behaviour or emotional state, e.g. result in poor concentration, tiredness, memory difficulties;
- when a TA has any uncertainty or concerns about the administration of medication to pupils that they check with parents/carers and/or health professionals before taking further action;
- when pupils may need regular access to asthma reliever inhalers or adrenaline injector pens, these should be readily available to them, and not be locked away;
- where pupils with medical needs are participating in educational visits and in out-of-school-hours' learning, staff supervising these should be fully aware of the child's medical needs, medication requirements and emerging procedures, as outlined in the pupil's healthcare plan;
- any pupils with medical needs taking part in sporting activities or PE may require immediate access to their medication, i.e. asthma inhalers, and these should be readily available as a precautionary measure before and/or during exercise;
- TAs should have access to protective disposable gloves if dealing with any spillages of body fluids from pupils, such as blood, and disposing of soiled dressings or used medical equipment such as syringes;
- where necessary, a TA accompanies a pupil taken to hospital by ambulance in an emergency and remains with the pupil until their parents/carers arrive.

5

Teaching Assistants Supporting Learners to Enjoy Learning and Achieve

Introduction

The chapter opens with what the *Every Child Matters* (ECM) outcome 'enjoy and achieve' entails. It provides TAs with a toolkit of a range of practical strategies that can be utilised when supporting pupils' personalised learning in achieving this ECM outcome, which complement the primary and secondary national strategies recommended approaches.

Enjoy and achieve

The ECM outcome 'enjoy and achieve' aims to enable learners to:

- be ready for school (positive attitude to learning and behaviour);
- attend and enjoy school (good attendance and enjoy learning);
- achieve stretching national educational standards at primary school;
- achieve personal and social development and enjoy recreation;
- achieve stretching national educational standards at secondary school.

The learning context

Learning is a dynamic, interactive, emotional and social process which requires the right conditions. These include the following:

- pupils coming from a home background where education and learning are valued and viewed positively;
- pupils having their basic needs met at home, e.g. safe, healthy, well-cared for, sufficient sleep;
- pupils learning in an appropriate learning environment, e.g. emotionally intelligent, stress-free, blame-free, secure, calm, welcoming classroom;
- pupils having positive, trusting, respectful relationships with adults and peers, at home and at school;
- pupils experiencing consistent and clear expectations for responsible behaviour, at home and at school.

Facts about learning

On average, learners remember:

- 20 per cent of what is read;
- 30 per cent of what is heard;
- 40 per cent of what is seen displayed;
- 50 per cent of what is said or explained to others;
- 60 per cent of what is done in practical work;
- 90 per cent if all the above multi-sensory methods are utilised in learning;
- 80 per cent of new knowledge is lost within 24 hours, without a review of learning;
- a learner's maximum concentration span on average is two minutes in excess of their chronological age, in minutes. For example:
  - a six-year-old's maximum time on task is six minutes, with a two to three minute break from task;
  - a ten-year-old's maximum time on task is 12 minutes with a two to five minute break from task;
  - an 11–12-year-old's maximum time on task is 15 minutes with a two to five minute break from task;
  - a 15–16-year-old's maximum time on task is 20 minutes with a two to five minute break from task;
  - an adult's maximum time on task is 20–25 minutes a two to five minute break from task.

The brain and learning

The brain functions best when it is exposed to the optimum conditions for learning which include:

- exercise through brain breaks which help the supply of oxygen and glucose to reach the brain;
- regular access to drinking water;
- a relaxed, calm learning environment free from emotional stress;
- a good supply of fish oils (Omega 3), iron and zinc-rich foods such as green leaf vegetables, fruit, nuts, fish and vegetable oil.

Brain facts

- at birth, most children have 100 billion active brain nerve cells;
- by eight months a baby's brain has 1,000 trillion connections;
- during the first three years of a child's life the foundations of thinking, language, vision, attitudes and aptitudes are laid down;
- the brains cerebral cortex grows most rapidly in the first ten years of a child's life;
- by ten years of age in the average child, half of the 1,000 trillion connections have died off;
- 50 per cent of an individual's ability to learn is developed in the first four years of life;
- another 30 per cent of an individual's ability to learn is developed by the age of eight;
- the final 20 per cent of an individual's ability to learn is developed by the age of 17;
- the adult brain weighs about 3 lbs;
- the brain is not designed for constant attention;
- smoking, alcohol and drugs in excess severely affect the growth and effectiveness of the brain.

Table 5.1 Differences between the male and female brain

Male brain	Female brain
• Boys develop the right side of their brain faster than girls, which results in them having better visual, spatial, logical and perceptual skills than girls. • The male brain has fewer connecting fibres between the left and right sides and is a more compartmentalised brain, which accounts for why men find it difficult to multi-task, unlike females. • The male brain is 9 per cent physically bigger than the female brain, but this does not make them cleverer than females, as both have the same number of brain cells. • The right side of the male brain is larger than the left side. • Males favour the right ear for listening. • The male brain shrinks by 20 per cent by the age of 50. • Boys are three times more likely to be dyslexic than girls. • Males are more frequently left-handed than females. • Males have a shorter attention span than females.	• Girls develop the left side of their brain more rapidly than boys, which results in them speaking sooner, reading earlier and learning a foreign language more quickly than boys. • Baby girls generally develop their corpus callosum earlier than boys, which accounts for why girls acquire language skills before boys. • The corpus callosum (the bundle of nerve fibres connecting the left and right sides of the brain together) are generally thicker in baby girls than baby boys, and results in women having up to 30 per cent more connections than men, between the two sides of the brain. • The left side of the female brain is larger than the right side. • Females listen with both ears. • The female brain does not shrink with age.

LEFT HEMISPHERE	RIGHT HEMISPHERE
Female	Male
Academic brain	Creative brain
Right side of body	Left side of body
Enjoy structured tasks	Enjoy open-ended tasks and self selected tasks
Clear instructions	Follows hunches and is impulsive
Written information	Artistic
Mathematical formula	Visual
Numbers	Pictures and images
Judgement of quantity	Imaginative
Logical	Perceptive
Verbal	Ideas
Words	Enjoys sport
Phonetic reading	Forms and patterns
Spelling	Dimension
Writing	Spatial manipulation
Language	Daydreaming
Facts	Visioning
Unrelated factual information	Fantasy
Deduction	Rhyme
Analysis	Rhythm
Practical	Musical
Order	Musical appreciation
Sequence	Tune of a song
Words of a song	Whole language reader
Lineal	Sees the big picture
Sees fine detail	Learns the whole first then the parts
Learning the parts to whole	

Figure 5.1 Left and right brain hemisphere characteristics.

The differences between male and female brains

It is useful for TAs to be aware of the differences between male and female brains, and to take account of these when tailoring and delivering appropriate strategies to support pupils' personalised learning. TAs, like teachers, need to engage pupils in learning activities that use both sides of the brain, even though traditionally the national curriculum has been biased towards left-brain activities.

Brain physiology

The corpus callosum which links both sides of the brain together, allows the left and right hemispheres of the brain to communicate and exchange information.

Prefrontal cortex – deals with thinking and emotions.
Anterior cingulate cortex – weighs up options, makes decisions and is the 'worry' centre.
Motor cortex – controls activity.
Temporal lobe – is the speech centre of the brain.
Insula – is the centre that processes gut feelings.
Parietal lobe – handles spatial ability.
Occipital lobe – is the visual centre of the brain.
The cerebellum – is the little brain which plays a key part in adjusting posture and balance.
The 'gatekeepers' – three in total: the amygdala, the hippocampus and the caudate nucleus relay important messages to the brain and are responsible for instinct and memory.

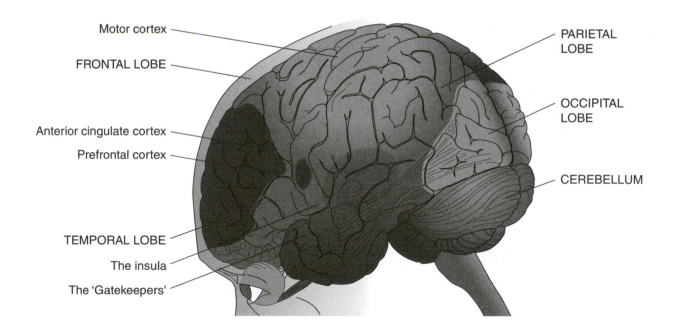

Figure 5.2 The component parts of the brain.

The brain's levels

Table 5.2 The brain's levels

Brain level	Types of activities	Outcomes
Level 1: Reptilian brain At the stem of the brain near the top of the neck	This controls the instinctive functions such as: breathing, heart rate, grasping, crawling, walking, reaching, turning, touching, pushing, pulling, movements of legs and arms.	Leads to: Hand–eye coordination Gross-motor skills Pre-writing ability
Level 2: Cerebellum The next level up from the reptilian brain	This is responsible for balancing and learned functions such as: spinning, swinging, rolling, tumbling, dancing, listening.	Leads to: Balance Sporting ability Riding a bicycle Fine motor coordination Typing or word processing Writing skills Reading skills
Level 3: Mammalian brain The next level up from the cerebellum	This controls the emotions and sexuality and has a key role to play in memory. It controls functions such as: stroking, cuddling, playing.	Leads to: Love Security Bonding Social skills Cooperation Confidence
Level 4: Cortex At the top of the brain and above the mammalian brain	This is used for thinking, talking, seeing, hearing and creating, assembling puzzles, recognising and making patterns, playing word games, repetitive play and appreciating music.	Leads to: Mathematics Logic Problem solving Fluent reading Spelling Good vocabulary Writing Painting Memory Musical ability

Source: Dryden and Vos 2001: 238.

The brain and dyslexia

A child who is born with dyslexia has both sides of the brain equally developed, resulting in less efficient nerve fibres between the right and left sides of the brain. This is different to non-dyslexic children whose left side of the brain (which develops language skills), is more developed than the right side of the brain.

This factor accounts for why dyslexic children, particularly boys, have great difficulty processing information, and struggle to acquire the language skills of reading, spelling and writing. They also experience difficulties with memory, coordination and time management. Learners with dyslexia benefit from the use of multi-sensory learning approaches, e.g. visual, auditory and kinaesthetic (VAK).

The learning cycle

The learning cycle, as part of personalised learning, should be evident in the delivery of teaching and learning, and support for learning. Teachers and TAs need to collaborate and plan together to ensure that the learning cycle becomes embedded as part of every day classroom practice.

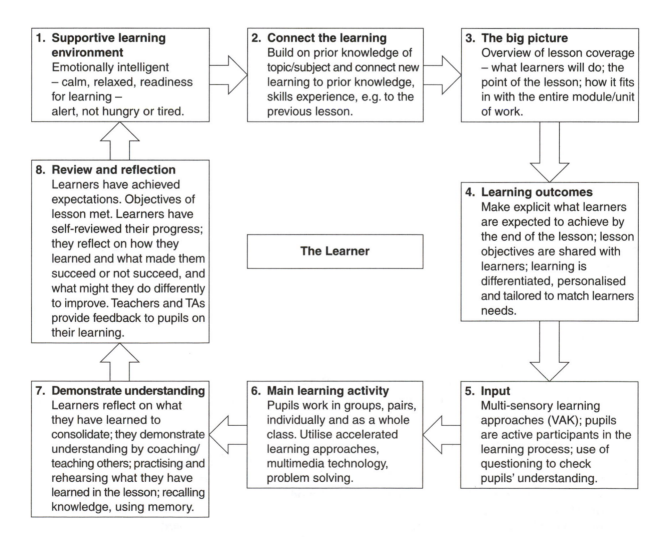

Figure 5.3 The learning cycle.

Learning styles

Learning styles refer to how pupils prefer to receive information; how they like to learn; and how they can get the best out of their learning.

Pupils learn in different ways. Teachers and TAs may teach in their own dominant preferred learning style, which can create barriers to learning for some learners who don't prefer to learn in that same way. This is why it is important for teachers and TAs to utilise a range of multi-sensory and accelerated learning approaches in order to ensure all learners fulfil their optimum potential. Personalised learning and learning styles go hand-in-hand. Table 5.3 illustrates the characteristics of four learning styles with some recommended teaching and learning support approaches that will ensure barrier free learning experiences for the full diversity of learners, i.e. from the less able to the most able, gifted and talented pupils.

Table 5.3 Learning styles

Auditory	Logical/theorists
CHARACTERISTICS Good listeners, fluent, expressive talkers; good vocabulary; explains things clearly to others; enjoys brainstorming; quick to learn from listening to others; sequences and organises information. *LEARNS LEAST WHEN:* Unclear guidance on how to do a task is given; or when information is repeated several times. *APPROPRIATE TEACHING AND LEARNING SUPPORT APPROACHES* Use audio tape or radio activities; provide opportunities to discuss in groups; give opportunity for oral feedback; use investigative reporting/ interviewing; provide opportunities for pupils to express ideas in their own words.	*CHARACTERISTICS* Enjoys knowing and applying theories, concepts, models, principles; likes logical explanations; enjoys estimating, problem solving, doing quizzes and puzzles; works through tasks in an orderly and methodical way; is able to identify connecting links. *LEARNS LEAST WHEN:* Feelings or emotions are involved, or tasks are ambiguous and unstructured, or they are 'put on the spot'. *APPROPRIATE TEACHING AND LEARNING SUPPORT APPROACHES* Provide step-by-step plans/instructions; use data in a variety of forms; provide a theory or principle to work from; give them time to explore ideas and think things through.
Visual	Kinaesthetic/activists
CHARACTERISTICS Observant; quick to see things others miss; photographic memory; good sense of direction; good at visualising events and information. *LEARNS LEAST WHEN:* Under time constraints, or when they can't see any relevance in the task, or when they don't spend enough time or pay attention to specific detail. *APPROPRIATE TEACHING AND LEARNING SUPPORT APPROACHES* Need time to watch and think things through; respond best to visual materials, video and websites; introduce flow charts/diagrams, mind maps and brainstorming; utilise picture sequencing; visualisation exercises; highlighting text; drawing to demonstrate their understanding of a text.	*CHARACTERISTICS* Enjoys teamwork; doing practical activities; has good coordination and manual dexterity; enjoys concrete experiences; learns by example, by demonstration and modelling; remembers by doing. *LEARNS LEAST WHEN:* Passive, or when work is solitary, or asked to attend to theory or detail; or, when information is presented orally or in writing. *APPROPRIATE TEACHING AND LEARNING SUPPORT APPROACHES* Provide opportunities to touch/manipulate objects; build models, participate in activity-based learning; investigation/experimental work.

Many schools are already tracking pupils according to their preferred learning styles on the basis of whether they are visual, auditory or kinaesthetic (VAK) learners. While it is useful to know what a pupil's preferred learning style is, learners need to experience all three VAK learning styles in a lesson. The importance and value of knowing what an individual pupil's preferred learning style is when they may be struggling to learn a skill or understand a concept, and the only way to enable the child to master this aspect of learning is by using the pupil's preferred learning style; or, where constantly working outside a pupil's preferred learning style leads to boredom, frustration and a lack of motivation. The preferred learning style that pupils adopt is often attributed to acquired habits in learning.

Transferring learning from intervention programmes

Many TAs are responsible for delivering targeted intervention and 'catch-up' programmes, particularly in literacy and numeracy. Where this is the case it is important that there is a focus on teaching and reinforcing the skills required to enable these pupils to participate more effectively within mainstream lessons. This will ensure that pupils begin to see the relevance of what they learn in an intervention or 'catch-up' programme, and therefore more readily transfer this learning across the curriculum.

TAs, during the delivery of intervention and catch-up programmes, need to ensure that they provide and model examples of when the pupils are likely to use and apply the knowledge and skills learned in these targeted programmes in different curriculum subject areas or contexts.

It is also important for TAs to feedback to the class/subject teacher what the pupil has covered in the intervention or 'catch-up' programme and what they have achieved, in order that the teacher can make a point of ensuring the pupils concerned can apply this learning and knowledge within the whole class learning context.

Questioning

Questioning accounts for up to one-third of all teaching and learning time, with teachers on average asking a class of pupils up to two questions every minute. The quality and type of questions asked is more important than the number of questions learners are asked in any lesson by teachers and TAs. A good quality open question poses a challenge that helps to extend a pupil's thinking.

The use of questioning is a key means of transferring knowledge, and leads to more effective learning. Questioning helps to motivate learners, to assess their learning, and to promote reflection, analysis and enquiry.

The purpose of questioning

The purpose of utilising questioning when supporting learners is to:

- ensure pupils are active, interested, alert, engaged and challenged participants in the learning process;
- help reveal any misunderstandings or misconceptions and to turn these into positive learning opportunities;
- assist pupils in reflecting on given information and to remember it;
- assist pupils in developing their thinking skills;

- promote reasoning, problem solving, evaluation and the formulation of hypotheses which are cross-curricular thinking skills;
- focus pupils' thinking on key concepts and issues;
- encourage pupils to discuss ideas;
- extend pupils' thinking from concrete and factual to the analytical and evaluative;
- enable teachers and TAs to check pupils' prior knowledge and their understanding;
- mobilise and recall existing knowledge and experiences to create new understanding and meaning;
- promote pupils' thinking about the way they have learned.

(DfES 2004f: 2–3)

Types of questions

Initially, there are two basic types of questions:

1   Closed lower order factual recall questions – these require pupils to remember, and have a single right answer, and help to check knowledge and understanding, e.g. what, who, when, or where.
2   Open higher order thought-provoking questions – these require pupils to think, and have a range of possible responses, e.g. how, why, which.

Practical strategies for TAs using questioning to support learning

- When supporting the learning of pupils TAs should ensure they utilise a combination of higher order and lower order questions in proportion of 50 per cent for each.
- Where appropriate, and dependent on the ability range of pupils being supported, it may be useful for TAs to model how to ask and answer questions with pupils.
- TAs need to use an appropriate waiting time to illicit pupils' responses to questions posed, for example: wait at least three seconds for the response to a lower order closed question, and ten seconds for a higher order open question response.
- Consider extending the waiting time beyond ten seconds to enable the learner to revise and expand upon their response, and to encourage other pupils to contribute.
- Wherever the opportunity arises, pose a higher order question at the end of a learning support or intervention session to stimulate pupils' thinking in readiness for discussion the next day.
- Keep pupils on task by asking quick-fire lower order open type questions.
- Where the TA knows that some pupils find answering questions a stressful process for fear of giving the incorrect answer, it is useful to ask questions that require a collective group response, rather than an individual pupil response.
- Personalise and tailor questions to match the ability of the learner, for example, differentiate the response level by giving less able pupils learning resources or curriculum materials to refer to for finding the answer, whereas, with more able pupils pose the question first without providing them with any curriculum materials to refer to.
- Ask pupils questions sequentially by starting off with lower order questions and building up to higher order questions.
- Ensure the learning environment is emotionally intelligent with a 'no-blame' culture, where it is OK to give an incorrect response to a question.

Asking good quality higher order questions in learning support time forms the basis for enabling pupils to become more successful, curious and flexible learners.

TA strategies for encouraging learners to ask questions

- Offer the group you are working with in-class, or in an intervention programme session, the opportunity to pose a range of questions related to the topic, that they would like answered in future lessons.
- Ask pupils to set questions at the end of a topic or session for other pupils in the group or class to answer, awarding praise or marks for the quality of the question posed rather than for the answer.
- Provide opportunities during support time to enable pupils to use the search engine on the internet to pose enquiries, working in a small group or in pairs, or individually.
- In partnership with the teacher you are supporting, create a question wall area in the classroom, where pupils, the teacher and the TA can post questions they would like to find the answer to, related to the topic.
- To enable more reticent pupils to ask questions, use a question box with 'post-it' notes to enable them to participate and be included.
- Ask pupils to bring a question related to the topic or concept being taught in smaller group support sessions to the next lesson.
- Consider having one or two key questions written down for the pupils you are supporting, and structure the learning support or intervention session around exploring the answers to these questions.
- Utilise hot-seating, where pupils take turns to be a character from history, literature or current affairs, and other pupils ask them questions related to the context.
- Challenge more able learners by providing them with the answer, and ask them to suggest what the question might have been.

Question terminology

It is useful for TAs to enable the learners they are supporting to understand the question terminology often used in external examinations and in national tests, in order that they provide the correct answers.

Account for – explain and examine the points related to the subject or topic.
Analyse – explore the main ideas of the topic or subject; show why they are important, and how they are related.
Compare – show the similarities.
Contrast – show the differences.
Describe – give a detailed and complete account of the subject or topic.
Differentiate – explore and explain the difference.
Discuss – explore the topic or subject by looking at the advantages and disadvantages, pros and cons, the arguments for and against, and attempt to reach some sort of overall judgement, opinion or conclusion.
Explain – make a topic clear, show the underlying principles, give illustrations and clear examples.
Interpret – explain the meaning by using examples and opinions.
List – give reasons or points one by one.
Outline – provide an overall view of the subject or topic. Include main points.
Summarise – give a brief account of the main points and attempt to come to some conclusion.
Trace – in chronological order describe how something has developed.

(Reid 2005: 152)

Questions that help pupils to assess their own learning

Listed below are some basic questions TAs may find helpful to use to support pupils' self-reviewing their own learning and progress.

- What have I learned?
- What have I found difficult?
- What do I need to learn next?
- What would help me to do better?

TAs can find further information related to questioning on the following websites:

www.youthlearn.org/learning/teaching/questions.asp
www.dmu.ac/uk/ffjamesa/teaching/questions_3a.htm
www.teachernet.gov.uk

(Insert 'interactive teaching' into the search engine on the teachernet website and it should provide a link to material on questioning.)

Table 5.4 Questioning to support thinking skills

Applying knowledge	Analysing understanding	Synthesising thinking	Evaluating
Can you explain why/how/which…? What would you have done…? What do you think will happen/would have happened next…? What makes you think…? What would you use for…?	How would you group/sort/categorise/classify? Can you work out the parts/features/structure of…? How can you show the differences/similarities of…? What patterns can you find…? What evidence can you find to…?	Can you think of a better way to…? What would you have done if…? How would you tackle this next time…? How would you change/adapt to make a new…? Given the choice, what would you do…?	How successful was…? How would you rate…? What do you think of…? What makes … good/bad/average?

Source: Smith 2007: 10.

Thinking skills

These are a series of cross-curricular skills that enable pupils to understand the processes of meaningful learning; how to think flexibly; and, how to make reasoned judgements. It entails learners in processing information, reasoning, enquiring, evaluating and thinking creatively, i.e. thinking 'outside the box'.

Table 5.5 gives an overview of Benjamin Bloom's hierarchy of thinking skills. TAs will find this provides them with a useful quick point of reference as to the types of activities pupils need to do, and what questions TAs and teachers need to ask pupils for each thinking skill.

Table 5.5 Bloom's hierarchy of thinking skills

Thinking skill objective	Definition with link to thinking	What pupils need to do		Examples of question prompts
6. Evaluation	The ability to judge the value of something using criteria to support the judgement. Evaluation questions expect pupils to use their knowledge to form judgements and defend the positions or viewpoints they take up. Evaluation demands very complex thinking and reasoning.	Appraise Argue Assess Critique Defend Evaluate Give opinion/viewpoint Grade Judge Justify Rate Recommend	Select	What do you think about…? What are your criteria for assessing? Which is more important/moral/logical…? What inconsistencies are there in…? What errors are there…? Why is the … valid…? How can you defend…? Why is the order important…? Why does it change? Why is it better?
5. Synthesis	The ability to re-form individual parts to make a new whole. Synthesis questions demand that pupils combine and select from available knowledge to respond to unfamiliar situations or solve new problems.	Arrange Be original Combine Compose Construct Create Design Forecast Formulate Hypothesise	Imagine Invent Organise Re-organise	What could we add to, improve, design, solve…? Propose an alternative… What conclusion can you draw…? How else would you…? State a rule… How do the writers differ in their response to…? What happens at the beginning of the story/poem and how does it change?
4. Analysis	The ability to understand how parts relate to a whole, and understand structure and motive. Analysis questions require pupils to break down what they know and reassemble it to help them solve a problem.	Analyse Break down Categorise Classify Compare and contrast Criticise Differentiate Discern fact from opinion Explore Infer Investigate	Question Relate Support Test	What is the evidence for parts or features of…? Separate fact from opinion. What is the function or purpose of …? What assumptions are being made and why? What is the evidence? State the point of view. Make a distinction between… What is this really saying? What does this symbolise?

Table 5.5 (*Continued*)

Thinking skill objective	Definition with link to thinking	What pupils need to do	Examples of question prompts
3. Application	The ability to transfer knowledge learned in one situation or context to another. Questions in this aspect require pupils to use their existing knowledge and understanding to solve a new problem or to make sense of a new context.	Apply to a new context Demonstrate Employ Interpret Model Predict Show how Solve Use	What other examples are there? What shape of graph are you expecting? What do you think will happen and why? Where else might this be useful? How can you use a spreadsheet to…? Can you apply what you now know to solve…? What does this suggest to you? How does the writer do this? What would the next line of my modelled answer be? How can you best demonstrate your understanding? If you did this again what would you do it differently?
2. Comprehension	The ability to demonstrate basic understanding of concepts and the curriculum, and translate this into other words. Comprehension questions require pupils to process the knowledge they already have in order to answer the question.	Edit Extend Explain Give examples Illustrate Report Restate Review Simplify Summarise Translate	What do we mean by…? Explain. How do you think…? Why do you think that…? What might this mean? Explain what a spreadsheet does. What are the key features of…? Explain your model. What is known about…? What happens when…? What word represents…? What is significant about…? Can you think of any other similarities? What do you consider essential…?

Table 5.5 (*Continued*)

Thinking skill objective	Definition with link to thinking	What pupils need to do	Examples of question prompts
1. Knowledge	The ability to remember something learned previously. Pupils will need to link aspects of knowledge necessary for a task to other relevant information.	Define Describe Find Identify Label List facts Locate Match Memorise Name Recall information Recite Remember Tell	Who, what, where, when, how? Describe what you see. . . What is the name for . . .? What is the best one. . .? Where in the book would you find . . .? What are the types of graph. . .? What are we looking for in . . .? Where is this set? What three things are the most important? List the key characters in the story.

Source: DfES 2004f: 13,19–20.

Notes

Key: Knowledge, Comprehension and Application are lower order thinking skills.

Analysis, Synthesis and Evaluation are higher order thinking skills.

Learners who are able to analyse, synthesise and evaluate, i.e. use the higher order thinking skills should attain National Curriculum level 5 and above, or GCSE Grade C and above.

Multiple intelligences

Howard Gardner, a psychologist, suggested individuals have different types of intelligences, or potential intelligences, which affect the way a learner prefers to learn. These are referred to as multiple intelligences (MI). Table 5.6 provides TAs with a useful overview of the multiple intelligences, which outlines the types of learning support activities that could be used for developing each type of intelligence. Ideally, TAs, like teachers, will wish to develop and widen pupils' repertoires of multiple intelligences, incorporating these as part of personalised learning.

Table 5.6 Multiple intelligences

Intelligence type	Characteristics	Examples of learning tasks and activities
Verbal–linguistic	A facility for words and language in speaking, reading and writing. Examples: journalists, editors, authors, poets	Discussion, group work, pair work, debates, interviewing, expositions, presentations, improvisations, listening to guest speakers, mnemonics, writing notes and essays, poems, sketches, stories, reading, brainstorming, word games; produce and edit school or class magazine
Logical–mathematical	A capacity for inductive and deductive thinking and reasoning, as well as for the use of numbers and the recognition of abstract patterns. Examples: engineers, accountants, mathematicians, scientists, lawyers, detectives	Puzzles, problem-solving tasks, predicting or hypothesising tasks, investigations, sequential tasks, summaries, pattern spotting, classifying and deducting, analysing and interpreting data
Visual–spatial	An ability to visualise objects and spatial dimensions, and to create internal images and pictures. Examples: architects, painters, navigators, chess players	Diagrams, charts, videos, films, graphs, posters, mind maps, pamphlets, textbooks, pictures, drawing, visualisation (creating mental pictures), collages, colour highlighting, displays, mime, use of computer graphics
Bodily–kinaesthetic	A high degree of control over physical motion; being adept with hands and enjoying active involvement in an activity. Examples: dancers, actors, athletes, surgeons, racing car drivers	Role play, drama, dance, model making, simulations, 'show-me' cards, freeze-frames, improvisation, associating ideas with movements, human graphs, human sentences or timelines, field trips, games, competitions
Musical–rhythmic	An ability to recognise tonal patterns and sounds; a sensitivity to rhythm, beat and melody. Examples: composers, conductors of orchestras, recording engineers, musical instrument makers, musicians	Chants, rhymes, songs, mnemonics, raps, poems, musical interpretations; work to music
Interpersonal	Strong social skills and relationships with others; being a sensitive listener. Examples: counsellors, teachers, politicians, personnel managers	Collaborative group work, pair or team work; interviewing, hot-seating, teaching or coaching others, peer tutoring

Table 5.6 *(Continued)*

Intelligence type	Characteristics	Examples of learning tasks and activities
Intrapersonal	An ability to be reflective and intuitive; a high degree of self-knowledge and self-reflection (meta-cognition), understanding one's own feelings. Examples: novelists, counsellors, philosophers	Individual research, learning journals, reflecting on own learning, identifying own questions, self-evaluation, personal diaries, solo study, independent learning
Naturalistic	Enjoyment of the outdoors; ability to work with and harmonise with nature; conducting own enquiries and making links between new learning and the natural world. The classification and understanding of the phenomena of nature. Examples: botanist, biologist, ecologist, naturalist, anthropologist, conservationist, farmer	Multi-sensory experiences, collecting and classifying data on species, creatures, flora and fauna; categorise and group phenomena; notice patterns in the natural world; analogies with natural world; observation, experiments, investigations, ecology and environmental studies
Existential (spiritual)	Sensitivity and capacity to tackle deep questions about human existence such as the meaning of life and why we die; what's going to happen to us in the future? Why are we here? Examples: philosopher, spiritualist	Debating and discussing philosophical issues; school philosophy club; study of ethics and moral education

Source: DfES 2004h: 59; DfES 2004: 14.

Howard Gardner has moved his thinking on and he considers learners in the twenty-first century need to develop five minds:

- Disciplined – acquire a real mastery of one or more disciplines.
- Synthesised – able to assess the huge amounts of information available and sort out what is valuable.
- Creative – able to innovate.
- Respectful – a notion going beyond mere tolerance.
- Ethical – able to act against self-interest, for the greater good.

According to Gardner, the most important of these minds is the ability to synthesise.

Mind mapping

The use of mind maps or concept maps was introduced to reduce note-taking and to help the quicker recall of information on a given topic. The technique is referred to as mind mapping because it replicates how the brain stores information by pattern and association. Mind maps utilise branches, pictures, colours and symbols to trigger and prompt the recall of information and facts. They help to organise, generate and present ideas in a simple visual way in order to improve understanding of information. They also help the learner to see relationships and connections between key concepts and ideas.

The process of devising a mind map to support pupils' learning

1 Place the concept, topic, question, idea or statement in the centre of a piece of paper in landscape format.

2 Using a tree branch format stemming from the central concept or topic, write on each main branch a key fact or point in one word related to the topic. You may use a symbol or picture instead of, or in addition to, a word, as a visual clue to help recall.

3 Create sub-branches off the main branches to record related points or details to support those on the main branches.

4 Make use of different colours for related topics to help link concepts and ideas.

5 Add to the mind map as knowledge about a topic is extended.

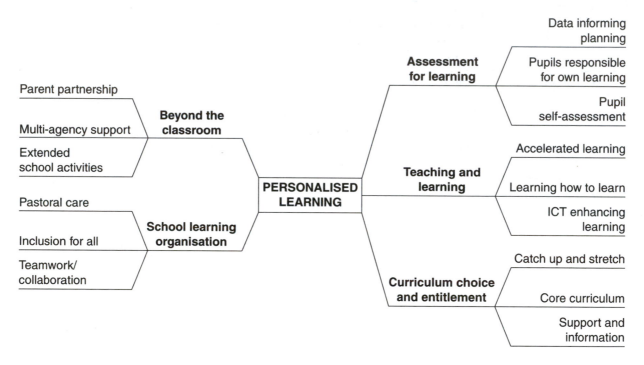

Figure 5.4 Example of a mind map.

Further information and examples of mind mapping can be found at:

www.mymindmap.net/Mind_Map_Templates.html
www.positivelymad.co.uk/al/mindmap_how.htm
www.jcu.edu.au/studying/services/studyskills/mindmap
www.mind-mapping.co.uk/mind-maps-examples.htm

TAs supporting learners during transfer and transition

Transfer (the move from one school or phase of education to another), and transition (the move from one year group to another within the same school or educational setting), can present some learners with immense challenges in coping with change. TAs have a valuable role to play in supporting transfer and transition. The following strategies will help TAs to ensure a smoother managed move for pupils requiring continued support for learning.

- Request quality time to meet the current TA in the pupils' year group, class or phase of education in order to gain a clear understanding as to which were the most effective learning support strategies and interventions utilised and which of these should be followed through into the next class or key stage.
- Make time to observe the pupils you are likely to support in the next academic year, working in their current class context. Focus on noting how they appear to learn best, how they work with and interact with staff and peers. Find out what aspects of learning the pupils find most difficult, and how they would like to be helped in the next class or school.
- Begin to compile learning profiles for pupils requiring TA support in the forthcoming academic year. These should identify their strengths and talents, favourite subjects, their preferred learning style, the strategies they identify as being most helpful to support their learning, and the aspects of learning they find difficult.
- Find out from the class teacher or the coordinator for personalised learning what attainment level pupils are operating at across the curriculum, wherever possible. This will help TAs to gain an insight into the level that curriculum materials may need to be differentiated to.
- Jointly, with the forthcoming class/subject teachers, begin to prepare and plan for incorporating accelerated learning approaches such as multiple intelligences, thinking skills, VAK, questioning, mind mapping as part of personalised learning that will ensure continuity and progression in learning for pupils.
- In negotiation with the senior staff member leading transfer and transition in your current school or educational setting, identify a critical group of learners who are most anxious about transition and transfer, and provide pre-transition/transfer small group intervention activities, as part of extended school provision.
- Monitor and feedback to current and previous class or form teachers on the success or otherwise of pupils' transition and transfer after one term or half a year in relation to progress and continuity in learning support.
- Where appropriate, seek pupil volunteers to talk to pupils in their previous class or year group, in relation to how they coped with transition and transfer in ensuring continuity in learning support.

Teaching assistants supporting gifted and talented learners

The revised National Occupational Standards for supporting teaching and learning in the classroom within the aspect of supporting pupils with additional needs, includes TAs supporting gifted and talented pupils. Gifted refers to those learners who are capable of excelling well ahead of their peers in one or more academic subjects, such as science, history or mathematics.

Talented learners are those who excel in areas of the curriculum that require creative skills, visual–spatial skills or practical abilities such as sport, PE, dance, drama, music or art and design.

Gifted and talented learners may excel in other areas of ability such as: leadership, creativity, problem-solving, thinking 'outside the box'. They are likely to work quickly, ask challenging questions and enjoy learning in different ways.

Gifted and talented learners may also have dual or multiple exceptionality (DME), i.e. are gifted or talented in a subject, but also have a special educational need such as a specific learning difficulty (dyslexia), or a sensory or physical impairment.

Every Child Matters expects all children and young people to reach their full potential. Gifted and talented learners are no exception, but some may underachieve because of adverse peer pressure. They may be bullied verbally in the form of name-calling: 'swot', 'boffin', or be physically bullied by peers because they are clever. They may also underachieve because their personalised learning provision does not challenge them sufficiently and they become bored, 'switch off' or misbehave.

Teaching assistants have been an under-used resource in relation to working with this group of learners in the past. The government's increased targeting and emphasis on improving provision for this group of pupils through the Primary and Secondary National Strategies, provides an excellent opportunity for TAs to support the learning and personal, social and emotional well-being of these learners, in partnership with teachers, and the leading teacher in gifted and talented education within the school.

Practical strategies for TAs supporting gifted and talented learners

Supporting personalised learning

- Utilise open-ended questioning when supporting in class, in order to encourage a deeper level of thinking.
- Provide opportunities to work with these pupils on developing their research skills, study skills, personal organisation and time management skills in order to enable them to become independent learners.
- Specifically teach them how to apply the higher-order thinking skills of analysis, synthesis and evaluation and the multiple intelligences in their learning, as you support them across the curriculum.
- Encourage gifted and talented pupils to record their ideas, thoughts, drawings, poems in their personal learning log throughout the day, in order to foster innovative and creative thinking.
- Tailor learning support to match the gifted and talented pupils' preferred learning styles, while ensuring they also experience multi-sensory learning approaches, i.e. visual, auditory and kinaesthetic (VAK).
- Make use of gifted and talented subject checklists to support the differentiation of curriculum materials to match their higher ability level.
- Where TAs are supporting and delivering extended school activities, at lunchtime or after school, e.g. clubs in drama, sports, chess or puzzles, ensure that gifted and talented pupils foster friendships with those peers who are not as gifted or talented as themselves.
- Support these learners in making best use of the internet for research, for example, teach them how to skim, scan, summarise and extract facts and information from text downloaded from websites.
- Make learning fun and challenging for these pupils, by incorporating puzzles, quizzes, role play, hot-seating, investigation and problem-solving during learning and study support.

Supporting gifted and talented learners' well-being

- TAs who are undertaking the role of pupil mentor/tutor or counsellor need to encourage these pupils to talk about their learning experiences or anxieties in an emotionally intelligent, secure, stress-free safe haven.

- When you hear other peers name-calling gifted and talented pupils for being clever, always challenge this immediately if the teacher has not heard this, and promote peers to respect and value individuals for their intellectual and physical abilities and differences.
- Provide support to those gifted and talented learners who value a quiet place, peace zone, safe haven in school, where they can unwind to soft music in a relaxing calm atmosphere. This will enable them to 'switch off' and give their over-stimulated brains a much needed rest.
- Tailor praise and recognition for gifts and talents appropriately to how the individual pupil prefers to receive this, e.g. public or private praise and acknowledgement.
- Utilise circle time with a small group of gifted and talented learners to build self-esteem and self-confidence, foster positive solution focused approaches to enable them to deal with any overt bullying from peers.
- Offer appropriate support to those gifted and talented pupils who may be finding it difficult to make friends with peers, through the use of pupil buddies, or teaching them social skills such as how to listen to others, tolerate others who are not as clever or talented as they are, or who may not work, learn or think as quickly as they do.
- Support gifted and talented pupils in coping with personal failure in not getting everything right first time.

Further information about supporting the learning and well-being of gifted and talented pupils can be accessed at the following websites:

www.nc.uk.net/gt
www.londongt.org/teacherTools
www.brookes.ac.uk/schools/education/rescon/cpdgifted/launchpads.html
gtwise.learnthings.co.uk
ygt.dcsf.gov.uk
www2.teachernet.gov.uk
www.standards.dfes.gov.uk/giftedandtalented

The website below provides guidance on dual or multiple exceptionality:

www.standards.dfes.gov.uk/primary/publications/inclusion/pns_gift_talent_dme_0006107

Teaching assistants as learning guides

Along with other members of the children's workforce, teaching assistants may take on the role of learning guide to pupils in secondary schools. The focus of the role is on how the pupil is progressing in their learning. As a learning guide the TA is expected to:

- know the pupil;
- know what the pupil is learning;
- understand the pupil's learning needs;
- jointly agree targets for learning with the pupil which are recorded on their individual learning plan;
- monitor pupil progress across a range of indicators which include the development of non-cognitive skills;
- meet with the pupil(s) regularly at least once every half term for an external formal session to review their learning needs;
- draw on resources and the knowledge of other practitioners to enable the pupil to progress in their learning;

- act as an advocate for the pupil within the school in the design of personalised learning and teaching experiences;
- move through the school with the pupil as a learning guide to promote continuity, particularly when the pupil is vulnerable or a LAC;
- provide a positive role model;
- use data to track pupil progress;
- meet with the pupil's parents/carers to discuss their child's overall progress and targets.

In conclusion, if learners as active participants in the learning process are given sufficient opportunities to develop and utilise accelerated learning approaches as a regular feature of personalised learning, they will be far more likely to enjoy their learning experiences and to achieve their full potential.

6

Teaching Assistants Supporting Learners to Make a Positive Contribution and to Achieve Economic Well-being

Introduction

The first part of the chapter focuses on what the *Every Child Matters* (ECM) outcome 'make a positive contribution' entails. It links this ECM outcome to the United Nations Charter on the rights of the child, and their views. It goes on to describe how teaching assistants (TAs) can support this aspect of learners' well-being, and in particular, ensuring that the voice of the child or young person is promoted and supported.

The second part of the chapter looks at the final ECM outcome 'achieve economic well-being'. It outlines how TAs can support this aspect of learners' well-being in the primary and secondary phase of education.

Make a positive contribution

The ECM outcome 'make a positive contribution' aims to enable learners to:

- engage in decision-making and support the community and environment;
- engage in law-abiding and positive behaviour in and out of school (understanding their rights and responsibilities);
- develop positive relationships and choose not to bully or discriminate;
- develop self-confidence and successfully deal with significant life changes and challenges;
- develop enterprising behaviour (involved in school and community activities).

Children and young people's views and rights

The organisation 4Children consulted a cross-section of 277 children and young people aged between three and 19 from across England in 2006. They found that:

- 78 per cent of children and young people aged from 5–19 valued being respected above all other qualities;

- 70 per cent of children and young people value adults who listen to them;
- 43 per cent of young people remembered teachers as having had a major impact on their lives;
- there was a direct relationship between age and the value accorded to caring, with children under five valuing caring qualities above all others.

(DfES 2006g: 16)

During 2006 and 2007 The Children's Society undertook *The Good Childhood Inquiry*. This sought the views of children and young people aged between five and 17 in the UK on six themes: friends, family, learning, lifestyle, health, and values. The final report and recommendations are due to be published during 2008. However, early findings from 11,000 young people aged 14–16 indicated:

- 29 per cent long for someone to turn to for advice and support;
- 93 per cent felt their parents/carers cared about them;
- 63 per cent felt that their parents/carers understood them;
- 7 per cent had been bullied or picked on often because of who they were;
- 60 per cent often hung about with their friends doing nothing in particular;
- 5 per cent admitted to having a drug problem;
- 8 per cent admitted to having a problem with alcohol;
- 49 per cent indicated there were no places for them to go in their area;
- 75 per cent liked living in their local area;
- 18 per cent did not feel safe when they were alone in their local area;
- 29 per cent felt that violence was a growing problem in their local area;
- 36 per cent felt that gangs were a growing problem in their area;
- 42 per cent indicated that their local area did not care about young people;
- 58 per cent were worried about their exams at school;
- 47 per cent often worried about school work;
- 78 per cent felt that life was worth living and had a sense of purpose.

(The Children's Society 2006: 10–18)

The findings will help to improve the lives of children and young people in the UK today, as well as informing future policy. TAs can view the findings from the research to date, on the following websites:

www.good.childhood.org.uk
www.mylife.uk.com

The convention on the rights of the child first came into force on 2 September 1990, as part of the United Nations Charter on Human Rights. There are 54 Articles of rights in total. A child is defined as any human being below the age of 18 years. TAs may find it useful to be aware of some of the Articles that align closely with the *Every Child Matters* outcomes, and in particular to 'making a positive contribution'. For example:

- Article 12 – the right to express their views freely in all matters affecting the child.
- Article 13 – the right to freedom of expression; this right shall include freedom to seek, receive and impart information and ideas of all kinds, regardless of frontiers, either orally, in writing or in print, in the form of art, or through any other media of the child's choice.
- Article 14 – respect the right of the child to freedom of thought, conscience and religion.
- Article 29 – the development of respect for human rights and fundamental freedoms; the preparation of the child for responsible life in a free society, in the spirit of understanding, peace, tolerance, equality of sexes, and friendship among all peoples, ethnic, national and

religious groups and persons of indigenous origin; and the development of respect for the natural environment.

- Article 31 – respect and promote the right of the child to participate fully in cultural and artistic life and shall encourage the provision of appropriate and equal opportunities for cultural, artistic, recreational and leisure activity.

The full convention of rights of the child can be accessed on the following website:

www.unhchr.ch/html/menu3/b/k2crc.htm

Teaching assistants supporting pupil voice

Teaching assistants provide valuable support in relation to enabling learners to make a positive contribution. They play an important role in the aspect of promoting pupil voice which helps to engage learners in decision-making, developing greater self-confidence, forming positive relationships with others and informing and participating in community activities.

What is pupil voice?

Pupil voice refers to pupil involvement and participation in them having more of a say, expressing their views and opinions about what they want in order to improve their learning and well-being in school. Pupil voice is not a new concept, and in 1991, Cullingford commented:

> [Pupils'] views deserve to be taken into account because they know better than anyone which teaching and learning styles are successful, which techniques of learning bring the best out of them and what the ethos of the school consists of.
>
> (Cullingford 1991: 2)

Why is pupil voice important?

The school self-evaluation form (SEF) requires school leaders to evaluate how they gather and act on the views of pupils. Pupil voice is important because every child and young person matters in a school and schools are for pupils. Pupils have rights and responsibilities that are underpinned by United Nations international legislation on human rights. If schools are going to change to meet the holistic needs of learners in the twenty-first century, then it is important that teaching and support staff, which includes TAs, listen to, respect and value the views of the pupils they work with.

Pupil voice often seeks views related to school policies, structures and organisation, school life and relationships with the community, parents/carers, school facilities, teaching and learning, curriculum provision, and the effects school provision has on the outcomes for learners.

The aims of pupil voice are to enhance learners' self-esteem and to enable them to become more successful lifelong learners. Pupil consultation enables learners to feel respected and to be treated in a more mature adult way. Pupil voice can take three forms:

- Authoritative – representing a particular group of learners, e.g. LAC, minority ethnic, gifted and talented.
- Critical – targeted at delivering a pupil's message to staff/adults who provide services to support their learning and well-being.
- Therapeutic – emphatic dialogue between pupils that reflects on issues and problems, e.g. peer mentoring schemes.

The level of pupil participation is illustrated in Table 6.1

Table 6.1 Levels of pupil participation

8. Pupil-initiated projects, where there are shared decisions with adults	The initial idea is conceived and identified by the pupils, who then work with adults as equal partners on this.
7. Pupil-initiated and directed	The original idea and the implementation of the idea have come from the pupils themselves.
6. Adult-initiated projects, sharing decisions with pupils	Adults involve pupils fully in the decision-making process.
5. Consulted and informed	The project is designed and run by adults, but the pupils understand the process and their opinions and views are treated seriously.
4. Assigned, but informed participation	Pupils understand the project or activity and volunteer to participate having had the purpose of the project made clear to them.
3. Tokenism	Pupils are given a voice but have had no choice about the subject, or how they will communicate about it, or any say in organising the occasion.
2. Decoration	Pupils are asked to participate in an event or activity but are not provided with any explanation as to the reason for their involvement.
1. Manipulation	Lowest level, pupils doing or saying what adults wish them to do, with no real understanding about the issue.

Source: Hadfield and Haw 2004.

Pupils can be consulted regularly through School Council meetings and classroom discussions as part of RE, PSHE and citizenship, or at the end of a module or unit of work. Occasional consultation is usually a one-off activity such as an annual pupil survey.

Methods of consulting pupils

TAs are often in the privileged position to hear pupils' views firsthand during their ongoing support for pupil learning and well-being. The method of consulting pupil voice is dependent on the scale of the enquiry, i.e. whether it is whole school or related to a particular class, form, year group or cohort. TAs can gather information on pupils' views by using:

- questionnaires and surveys;
- learning logs and diary entries;
- individual or small focus group interviews;
- school Council meetings;
- digital photographic evidence of school views;
- audio or video recordings of pupil interviews/discussions;
- emailing or text messaging;
- posting written views in suggestion boxes in school;
- force field analysis.

Figures 6.1 and 6.2, and Table 6.2, provide useful models of some of the above approaches, to enable TAs to gather the views of learners.

Three factors or changes that will improve pupil well-being in school:

- Extension of pupil counselling service, to include peer counsellors
- Exploring the creation of more quiet areas around school for pupils
- Exploring sound-proofing the dining area and making it a more pleasant and relaxing environment by introducing calming music, and introducing two lunchtime sittings

Figure 6.1 Example of pupil force field analysis.

Please answer the following questions as fully as you can.
You can record your answers in a format that you prefer, e.g. handwritten, word processed or emailed.

Year group: ....   **Form/class:** ....   **Date:** ....

Consultation topic: community/environment pupil participation

Questions

1. What school activities have you taken part in this year that have helped to improve the local community or environment?

2. How do you know the activity(s) you took part in have improved the local community/environment or helped members of the community?

3. What three things have you learned from taking part in a community-related or environmental activity?

   -

   -

   -

4. What other future school activities would benefit or help to improve the local community and the surrounding environment?

5. How much time would you be willing to give to a future community or environmental project next year?

   ☐ One hour a week after school for one term (eight weeks)

   ☐ Three hours on a Saturday morning every month

   ☐ One Friday afternoon every half term in school time

Thank you for answering the questions on this pupil survey.
Please post your completed survey in the post box in the main school entrance.

Figure 6.2 Model pupil community participation survey.

Table 6.2 *Every Child Matters* model pupil well-being log

This well-being log belongs to:

Class/Form:

The five Every Child Matters well-being outcomes are:

 Being healthy

 Staying safe

 Enjoy learning and achieving

 Positive contribution

Achieving economic well-being

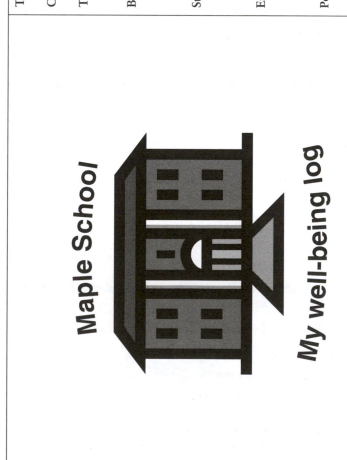

Maple School

My well-being log

Table 6.2 (*Continued*)

Being healthy	Staying safe
Put a ✓ in the relevant box/boxes	Put a ✓ in the relevant box/boxes
How do you keep healthy in school? exercise, PE, sport ☐ eating and drinking healthily ☐ keeping hands clean ☐ manage own feelings ☐	**How do you keep safe in school?** report bullying ☐ learn and play safely ☐ keep away from unsafe areas ☐ report any strangers to staff ☐
What else do you need to do to stay healthy in school? _____	What else do you need to do to keep safe in school? _____
What do you do to have a healthy lifestyle outside school? _____	What do you do to keep safe outside school? _____
Who can help you to stay healthy? (a) at school? _____ (b) at home? _____	Who can help you stay even safer? (a) at school? _____ (b) at home? _____
What is your personal target for being healthy? _____	What is your personal target for staying safe? _____
How will you achieve this target? _____	How will you achieve this target? _____

Table 6.2 *(Continued)*

Enjoying learning and achieving

Put a ✓ in the relevant box/boxes

How do you enjoy learning and achieving in school?

| learning in a group or pair ☐ | using favourite learning style ☐ | present work in other way to writing ☐ | value help of staff ☐ |
| enjoy going to school ☐ | like learning new things ☐ | behaving sensibly ☐ | attend school clubs ☐ |

What else do you need to do to enjoy learning and achieve in school?

_____

_____

What do you do to enjoy learning and to achieve outside school?

_____

_____

Who can help you to learn and achieve
(a) at school? _____
(b) at home? _____

What is your personal target for enjoying learning and achieving?

_____

How will you achieve this target?

_____

_____

Making a positive contribution

Put a ✓ in the relevant box/boxes

How do you make a positive contribution in school

| express views to School Council ☐ | helping others ☐ | partake in school events ☐ | school prefect ☐ |
| study buddy ☐ | sensible citizen ☐ | form/class representative ☐ | partake in after school clubs ☐ |

What else do you need to do to make a positive contribution in school?

_____

_____

What do you do to make a positive contribution at home and/or in the local community?

_____

_____

Who can help you to make more of a positive contribution
(a) at school? _____
(b) at home/in the community? _____

What is your personal target for making a positive contribution?

_____

How will you achieve this target?

_____

_____

Table 6.2 *(Continued)*

Achieving economic well-being

Put a ✔ in the relevant box/boxes

How do you achieve economic well-being in school?

| team working □ | making sensible decisions □ | looking for new chances □ | manage money □ |
| use ICT □ | idea about a career □ | solve problems □ | |

What else do you need to do to achieve economic well-being in school?

_____

_____

What do you do to achieve economic well-being outside school?

_____

Who can help you to achieve economic well-being
(a) at school? _____
(b) at home? _____

What is your personal target for achieving economic well-being?

_____

How will you achieve this target?

_____

Self-review of the five well-being outcomes

Rate your overall progress in achieving the five well-being outcomes on a scale 1–3
(1 = a little progress; 2 = average progress; 3 = good progress)

Being healthy □	Making a positive contribution □
Staying safe □	Achieving economic well-being □
Enjoying learning and achieving □	

Which well-being outcome do you need to improve in the most?

_____

_____

What will you need to do to enable you to achieve this well-being outcome?

_____

Who can help you to achieve this well-being outcome
(a) at school? _____
(b) at home? _____

My overall main personal well-being target is:

_____

Date of self-review _____

Signature _____

Principles underpinning pupil consultation

Where TAs are supporting teachers in pupil consultation, or leading pupil voice activities, the following principles will reassure learners that their views are valued and important in making things better in school for pupils.

- Explain participation in consultation is voluntary and not compulsory and that pupils will not be disadvantaged if they choose not to participate.
- Clarify the purpose and reason for pupil consultation and who is seeking their views.
- Confirm confidentiality and that responses will be anonymous.
- Explain your role as TA in supporting pupil consultation, e.g. acting as a neutral, impartial listener and recorder of pupil responses.
- Emphasise that responses to consultation questions should be general and not name specific staff.
- Inform pupils about what will happen to the information gathered from consultation.
- Confirm that feedback will be provided to pupils on the outcomes of consultation.

Further information about pupil voice can be found on the following websites:

www.standards.dfes.gov.uk/research/themes/pupil_voice
www.pupil-voice.org.uk
www.consultingpupils.co.uk

The benefits of Personal, Social and Health Education (PSHE)

Teaching assistants (TAs) may provide in-class support to learners during PSHE lessons, which help pupils to develop socially and emotionally. This subject enables learners to develop many of the skills and attributes featured in the ECM outcome: 'make a positive contribution'. In particular, PSHE helps learners to:

- develop and increase their self-confidence, self-reliance and self-esteem;
- know right from wrong when making decisions and responsible choices;
- be able to cope with life changes and new challenges;
- understand and respect difference and diversity in others;
- develop positive relationships with peers and adults;
- understand their own feelings and emotions as well as those of others;
- develop and maintain a healthy lifestyle and good emotional well-being;
- keep safe and consider the safety of others.

The PSHE programme within a school enables learners to transfer the skills and knowledge gained from the subject across the curriculum. TAs during in-class support can observe and feed back to teachers on how learners are taking initiative, contributing to decision-making, and making positive contributions overall in lessons, and to school life in general.

Practical strategies to support making a positive contribution

TAs, in partnership with teachers, utilising personalised learning approaches can support learners in PSHE, and across the curriculum, by utilising the following familiar support strategies:

- where appropriate, use social stories or poems to depict emotions and feelings that learners can relate to;

- role play and use drama activities to act out feelings, and model the appropriate responses and reactions learners can adopt to emotions such as anger, jealousy or grief;
- model coping strategies learners can adopt in order to help them deal with unfamiliar situations or sudden changes in routine, e.g. slow deep breathing, thinking about a more pleasant experience/memory;
- active listening to enable learners to feel confident in sharing feelings or concerns with TAs and teachers open and honestly, e.g. through circle time, circle of friends, negotiation and discussion;
- provide cooperative learning activities which will help to develop team working, and promote interpersonal skills and social interaction with peers, e.g. talking partners/elbow partners; group activities using investigative journalism, producing a news bulletin on a topical community or global issue, which makes good use of multimedia technology in its production, i.e. video recorders and digital cameras, audio recorders, pod-casting, powerpoint presentations;
- establishing a Youth Parliament or courtroom scenario to develop learners' moral judgements;
- support learners in participating in fund raising and mini-enterprise activities, as well as in voluntary work within the local community.

Teaching assistants supporting School Council activities

A School Council provides a forum for pupils to express their views about learning, well-being, aspects of school life, as well as community and environmental issues. School Councils are an excellent vehicle for enabling pupils to achieve the *Every Child Matters* outcomes.

Table 6.3 will assist teaching assistants to identify the types of School Council activities aligned with the skills pupils acquire, that enable learners to meet the five *Every Child Matters* outcomes.

TAs may be supporting pupils to make positive contributions in School Council meetings or in related School Council/form activities. This may entail TAs in partnership with class/form teachers, undertaking pupil surveys or supporting and promoting class discussions through the use of open questioning, and helping learners to record and collate their views. TAs may help pupils to analyse findings from these surveys, and publish the findings in school newsletters, on the school website, or on noticeboards around the school.

The impact of initiatives and improvements suggested by pupils will need to be evaluated by them. TAs can support pupils in demonstrating measurable outcomes. For example, *'the new playground equipment pupils requested and fund raised for, has resulted in 75 per cent of pupils using this, and 85 per cent of pupils consider the improved outdoor play facilities have made playtime more interesting and fun'.*

Further information about School Councils can be found at the following website:

www.schoolcouncils.org

Table 6.3 School Councils and the *Every Child Matters* outcomes

ECM outcome	School Council activities	Skills developed
Be healthy	• Enhancing sports and play facilities and promoting sports opportunities at school • Ensuring healthy eating options promoted and provided in school at lunchtimes and break, and in the breakfast club • Improving the quality of the school environment for learning, relaxation and well-being	• Confidence • Emotional well-being • Communication • Leadership • Building positive relationships • Negotiation • Mutual respect and tolerance
Stay safe	• Contributing to informing the school's anti-bullying scheme • Improving general safety in and around the school environment • Improving systems for pupil welfare and safeguarding (pastoral care) within the school	• Leadership • Openness and trust • Emotional intelligence • Conflict resolution • Cooperation • Empathy and caring for others
Enjoy and achieve	• Improving recreation facilities in and around school • Improving teaching, learning and curriculum provision • Informing extended services as part of extended school provision for pupils • Enhancing accessibility to learning and recreation activities for physically disabled children and adults	• Active listening • Diplomacy • Communication • Confidence • Self-worth • Respect of diversity and difference in others • Enquiry and investigation • Problem solving • Leadership
Make a positive contribution	• Improving the school and local environment, e.g. recycling, conservation projects • Developing and updating school rules and behaviour policy • Informing Youth Parliament and Youth Democracy	• Decision making • Consultation • Building positive relationships • Self-confidence • Solution focused problem solving • Respect • Negotiation
Achieve economic well-being	• Contributing ideas for community projects and initiatives • Enhancing work experience opportunities • Informing Careers programmes and support • Enhancing Enterprise Education opportunities, e.g. fund raising, mini-enterprise projects, budget planning	• Trust • Building productive relationships • Decision making • Confidence • Organisation • Problem solving • Change management • Risk taking • Team working • Action planning • Financial literacy • Negotiation • Investigation

Source: adapted from School Councils UK 2006. The extended and original version of the *School Councils and Every Child Matters* document can be viewed at: www.schoolcouncils.org/resources/free-downloads#ECM.

Teaching assistants supporting learners to achieve economic well-being

The *Every Child Matters* outcome 'achieve economic well-being' aims to enable learners to:

- engage in further education, employment or training on leaving school (acquire basic literacy, numeracy and ICT skills);
- be ready for employment (develop self-confidence and team-working skills);
- live in decent homes and sustainable communities;
- have access to transport and material goods;
- live in households free from low income, becoming financially literate.

Extended schools

The extended school initiative provides a core offer of services and activities beyond the school day to help meet the needs of its pupils and their families and the wider community. Extended school activities make significant contributions to enabling children, young people and their families to achieve the *Every Child Matters* outcomes, and in particular to achieve economic well-being.

Acting as local community hubs for lifelong learning and well-being, the core offer of services, which can be available in one school, or between a cluster of schools, includes the following:

- high quality wraparound childcare available from 8am to 6pm;
- a varied menu of activities such as study support, sport, dance, drama, arts and crafts, volunteering, business and enterprise activities, homework clubs, 'catch-up' and 'stretch' activities;
- parenting support which includes parenting programmes, family learning sessions, information for parents;
- swift and easy referral to a wide range of specialist support services, such as speech therapy, child and adolescent mental health services (CAMHS), intensive behaviour support, sexual health services, family support services;
- providing wider community access to ICT, sports and arts facilities including adult learning.

Teaching assistants make significant contributions to extended school service provision by running breakfast clubs and after-school clubs such as study support and homework clubs, as well as special interest clubs.

The *Every Child Matters* (ECM) outcome to achieve economic well-being is a developing area of school life, where some aspects of the outcome such as living in decent homes, and access to transport and material goods, are not directly influenced by school provision. However, through the PSHE and citizenship curriculum, as well as the numeracy/mathematics curriculum, pupils in the primary and secondary phases of education are taught about financial literacy, which includes:

- how to look after their money;
- keeping their money safe;
- how to save money;
- planning and budgeting.

Work-related learning and careers education is a major focus in secondary schools. Primary schools engage with this aspect of the ECM outcome by: engaging people from a range of jobs visiting the school and talking about their work, and also taking pupils to visit different workplaces. Mini-enterprise activities, and business and industry days in primary and secondary schools also help to develop pupils knowledge and skills in economic well-being.

Life coaching to support learners' economic well-being

Experienced teaching assistants (TAs), along with learning mentors, may explore the potential to seek training to become a life coach to support the economic well-being of those learners who may be underachieving, at risk of disaffection, or who have low self-esteem and lack motivation.

Although life coaching has been utilised usually with adults, the approach is beginning to be introduced into schools for use with pupils at secondary phase.

What is life coaching?

Life coaching is a holistic, solution focused, tailored and customised approach for motivating the personal and career development of individual targeted pupils.

What are the benefits of life coaching?

TAs undertaking the role of a life coach can help learners to:

- identify and develop their hidden talents;
- minimise their self-doubt;
- increase their self-awareness and self-reliance;
- improve and boost self-esteem, self-confidence, self-worth and self-image;
- unlock and realise their potential to fulfil aspirations and dreams;
- move their thinking forward;
- clarify future goals;
- enhance communication skills;
- improve relationships;
- make rational decisions;
- successfully manage change in their lives, e.g. transition from school to employment or training;
- reassess and organise their lives.

What does the life-coaching process entail?

In partnership with the pupil, the life coach examines the learners current situation, draws up an agreed action plan, and works with the pupil on an individual basis or in a small group, asking them questions to enable them to find their own solutions.

The TA as the pupil life coach or learning guide meets weekly with the pupil. They act as a confidential sounding board, where the learner can openly discuss their fears, frustrations, self-doubt, disappointments and achievements. There is a focus on moving the pupil from where they currently are in their personal life to where they want to be in the future, by helping them to identify what they need to do to reach their personal goal in order to achieve economic well-being in the future.

Further information about life coaching and related training can be found on the following websites:

http://www.endeavourct.ie/what-is-life-coaching.php
http://evolve-intl.com/3.html

Emotional well-being and social mobility

The National Children's Homes (NCH) research report entitled: *Emotional Wellbeing and Social Mobility – a New Urgency to the Debate*, published on the 20 June 2007, revealed that children's emotional well-being has a major impact on the emotional and social skills that enable a child and young person to gain a good education, qualifications and employment, as well as improving their life chances, i.e. achieve future economic well-being.

The report findings revealed that emotional well-being was considered to be more important than ability, physical health, family income, where a person lived and social class.

The NCH research report concluded that:

> The emotional wellbeing of children and young people in the UK seems to be deteriorating – children's personal interactions are declining, drug and alcohol misuse is rising, mental health is deteriorating, and anti-social behaviour and conduct disorder are on the increase.
>
> (NCH 2007a: 1)

In view of these social pressures that children and young people face in the twenty-first century, it is therefore crucial that TAs, along with other adults in school who work with vulnerable pupils, provide positive role models.

Ofsted judging economic well-being

Ofsted will seek evidence to exemplify learners achieving economic well-being across the curriculum, during inspection. TAs during their support of teaching and learning in the classroom are well placed to record from observation how well learners:

- take initiative;
- work in teams; and
- show responsibility and maturity.

7

Monitoring and Evaluating the Impact of Teaching Assistant Support and Interventions on ECM Outcomes for Pupils

Introduction

Any monitoring and evaluation activities undertaken by the school in relation to judging the impact of TA support on improving the ECM outcomes for pupils, should support the school's own self-evaluation and development planning process.

While it is important to systematically monitor and evaluate the impact of TA support on pupils' attainment, achievements, ECM well-being outcomes, access to the curriculum and out of school hours learning activities, their self-esteem, self-confidence, attitudes and motivation towards learning, it is also crucial that the effectiveness of the deployment of TAs throughout the school is monitored and evaluated by the senior leadership team.

In view of the increased focus on self-evaluation, personalised learning and the ECM outcomes, school leaders need to be demonstrating clearly how they engage TAs in feeding evaluative evidence of the impact of their support and interventions into the school self-evaluation form (SEF).

Prior to exploring monitoring and evaluation in greater depth with TAs, it is helpful at this stage to clarify the meaning of the two terms.

Monitoring

Monitoring refers to the ongoing process of gathering information to check the progress made in TA support and interventions for improving pupils' learning and ECM well-being outcomes, against objectives and targets set; identifying any trends in pupil performance and ECM outcomes; seeking the views of pupils, staff and parents/carers on TA support; checking that appropriate TA support strategies for ECM and personalised learning have been implemented.

Evaluation

Evaluation is concerned with judging the quality, effectiveness, strengths and weaknesses of TA support and interventions on pupils' learning and ECM well-being outcomes, by analysing quantitative and qualitative evidence collected from review and monitoring processes.

Evaluation of the impact of TA support on pupils' outcomes, helps to inform future planning and decision-making, in relation to how best to deploy TAs for *Every Child Matters* and personalised learning. Care must be taken when evaluating the impact and effectiveness of TA support on pupils' outcomes; improvements may not be attributed solely to TA support and interventions, as there may be other professionals and front-line workers from external agencies and organisations involved in removing barriers to learning and well-being, as part of a continuum of flexible personalised provision for targeted pupils.

Teaching assistant self-reflection activity

Reflect and think about the range of support and interventions you provide, which help to improve pupils' learning and ECM well-being outcomes. Answer the following questions to help you identify if there are any aspects of your support that could be further improved, or where you may require additional professional development opportunities, in order to better equip you to meet particular aspects of personalised learning and *Every Child Matters*.

- How well am I doing in relation to the support and interventions I deliver to help remove barriers to learning and improve ECM outcomes for the pupils I work with?
- What more could I aim to achieve in relation to improving the support I offer for learning and well-being, and what must I do to make this happen?
- How will I know if my support and interventions have been successful in improving learning and ECM well-being outcomes for the pupils I work with?
- How can I ensure that the evidence of the impact of my support and interventions as a TA are fed into the school's self-evaluation form (SEF)?
- When is the best time in the school year to review the impact of my TA support, and how should this be undertaken, and who with?
- Am I deployed appropriately to support pupils' learning and well-being? If not, how could my deployment be improved, in order to increase my effectiveness?

The TA self-reflection activity provides a good focused starting point for the completion of any formal monitoring and evaluation grids, such as the model provided in Table 7.1.

Teaching assistants tracking pupil progress
Why do TAs need to track pupil progress?

TAs need to track pupil progress in the aspects of personalised learning and ECM well-being outcomes in order to judge whether pupils:

- are on track to meet their personal learning and well-being targets set;
- make sufficient and good enough progress in relation to their prior achievements, attainment (value added progress), taking into account any contextual issues, as well as the frequency, nature and level of TA support and intervention provided.

TAs are advised to use their knowledge of the pupil, in addition to their own professional judgement of progress made, based on the Ofsted criteria descriptors for learning and well-being.

Table 7.1 Monitoring and evaluating the impact of teaching assistant support

Nature of TA support and interventions for learning and well-being	Impact of teaching assistant support and interventions on improving the *Every Child Matters* outcomes for pupils			
	Be healthy	Stay safe	Enjoy and achieve	Make a positive contribution	Achieve economic well-being

How often should TAs track pupil progress?

It is good practice to track the progress of pupils being supported at least at the end of every term, in the aspects of personalised learning and the ECM well-being outcomes.

How can the tracking information be used?

The TA needs to share the tracking data with the class/subject teacher(s) they support and work with, as it will contribute to informing future teacher planning and complement pupil level curriculum related attainment data. The tracking data for personalised learning and ECM well-being outcomes will contribute quantitative information to the school SEF, indicating the effectiveness of TA support and interventions.

School self-evaluation

School self-evaluation is a reflective, collaborative, analytic process rooted in the daily work of the school and classroom, which is central to driving school improvement. Good self-evaluation leads to improved outcomes for pupils. The views of a wide range of stakeholders help to inform self-evaluation.

The findings from self-evaluation help to inform priorities in school development planning. Where self-evaluation is integral to the culture of the school, stakeholders at all levels are committed to it and become fully involved. For example, TAs trained to analyse the results of tests and ECM outcomes data are able to identify more readily pupils who require extra support. Following additional support and interventions, TAs can undertake further analysis and self-evaluation to check that the support has improved pupils learning and/or well-being outcomes.

Ofsted commented:

> Pupils' achievement – the standards that they reach and their progress – is always at the heart of self-evaluation. It is a key element of the *Every Child Matters* (ECM) agenda. The school understand how well their pupils are doing because they rigorously track the personal development and academic progress of individuals, particular groups and cohorts of pupils. In this way they identify potential problems at an early stage and act upon them swiftly to counteract underachievement, poor behaviour and unsatisfactory attitudes to learning.
>
> (Ofsted 2006b: 5:14)

The school self-evaluation form (SEF)

The school self-evaluation form (SEF) is a summary of the outcomes of a school's self-evaluation process. It records annually the school's view of itself and how well it is doing, by providing key information and evaluative evidence that demonstrates the added value and impact of the actions implemented in raising standards and improving outcomes for pupils.

TAs need to select a good range of robust telling evidence for the school's SEF, that clearly demonstrates the value they have added, while specifying briefly the key TA support activities that have had the greatest impact on improving pupils' learning and ECM well-being outcomes. TAs should be conscious of the ECM outcomes throughout their evaluation and reflect this in the school's SEF. TAs need to consider carefully what difference their provision and support has made, and how they know this. The SEF in Part A evaluates progress against the Ofsted inspection schedule and focuses on:

Table 7.2 TA tracking sheet for personalised learning and ECM well-being outcomes

TERM: _____

TA: _____

UPN or pupil name	DOB	Ethnicity	Attendance	Assessment for learning	Teaching, learning and ICT	Curriculum entitlement, choice and access	School organisation for learning	Beyond school/ classroom	Be healthy	Stay safe	Enjoy and achieve	Positive contribution	Achieve economic well-being

Notes to Scores (Based on the Ofsted grades: 1 = outstanding; 2 = good; 3 = satisfactory; 4 = inadequate). Using the Ofsted judgement criteria, place an appropriate score for each pupil you support, related to the five aspects of personalised learning and the five *Every Child Matters* outcomes.

Table 7.3 Evaluating personalised learning

Ofsted grade	Features of personalised learning
Outstanding (1) (Exceptional, highly effective and worth disseminating beyond the school)	• Almost all learners make considerably better progress than might be expected, as a result of the very good teaching and TA support. • Learners behave very well and are engrossed in their work. • The excellent relationships between pupils and their teachers/TA are most conducive to learners' personal development. • The health and safety of learners is not endangered during learning activities. • Teaching and support for learning is based upon an expert knowledge of the curriculum, and is stimulating and rigorous. • The work is sensitively matched to the needs of individuals, and teachers' and TAs' high expectations ensure that all learners are challenged and stretched, whatever standard they are working at. • Teaching methods are imaginatively selected to deliver the objectives of the lesson, no time is wasted and teaching assistants and resources are well directed to support learning. • Assessment of learners' work successfully underpins the teaching and support for learning, and learners have a clear idea of how to improve.
Good (2) (Above average, effective and worth reinforcing and developing)	• Most learners make good progress and show good attitudes to their work, as a result of the good effective teaching and learning support they receive. • Behaviour overall is good and any unsatisfactory behaviour is managed effectively by teachers and TAs. • Learners are keen to get on with their work in a secure and friendly environment in which they can thrive. • The health and safety of learners are not endangered. • Provision is good for literacy, numeracy and ICT across the curriculum. • Teaching and support for learning is well-informed, confident, engaging and precise. • The teachers' and TAs' good subject knowledge lends confidence to their teaching styles and learning support strategies, which engage learners, and encourage them to work well independently. • The curriculum provides enrichment and good opportunities for all learners to progress and develop well, and is responsive to local circumstances. • Those pupils with additional learning needs have work well matched and tailored to their needs, based upon a good diagnosis of them. • Work is well matched to the full range of learners needs, so that most are suitably challenged. • The level of challenge stretches without inhibiting. • Teaching and learning support methods are complementary, are effectively related to the lesson objectives, and to the needs of learners. • Assessment of learners work by teachers and TAs is regular and consistent and makes a good contribution to their progress. • Accurate assessment informs learners how to improve. • Learners are guided to assess their work themselves. • Teaching assistants and resources are well deployed and directed to support learning. • Good relationships support parents/carers in helping learners to succeed. • Learners have many opportunities to contribute to and take on responsibilities in the community.

Table 7.3 (*Continued*)

Ofsted grade	Features of personalised learning
Satisfactory (3) (Average and adequate, but scope for improvement)	• Most learners make at least satisfactory progress and no major group fails to do so as a result of teaching and learning support. • Behaviour is generally satisfactory and, even where a minority are disruptive, this is not sufficient to cause the progress of most learners to be unsatisfactory. • The majority of learners are sufficiently motivated to continue working at an adequate pace throughout the lesson. • The tone of the lesson provides a satisfactory basis for the learners' continued personal development. • The health and safety of the learners' are not endangered. • Teaching and learning support is accurate, based upon a secure knowledge of the curriculum. The work is geared to the needs of most learners, although some might do better if given extra or different tasks. • The methods are soundly matched to the objectives, but are not particularly imaginative or engaging. • Adequate use is made of teaching assistants and resources, but there are ways in which their deployment could be more effective. • Not too much time is lost. • Teacher and TA assessment of learners' work is reasonably regular, but could be more supportive.
Inadequate (4) (Very ineffective, well below average and immediate radical change and action required)	• Learners generally, or particular groups of them, do not make adequate (less than satisfactory) progress because the teaching and learning support is unsatisfactory. • Learners do not enjoy their work and have an unsatisfactory attitude. • Behaviour is often inappropriate and not adequately or effectively managed by teachers or TAs. • The tone of the lesson does not promote the development of learners' personal qualities. • The health and safety of learners is endangered. • Provision is weak for literacy, numeracy and ICT. • The curriculum is inadequately matched to learners' needs, interests and aspirations, and excludes significant groups of learners, e.g. gifted and talented, ethnic minorities. • Teachers' and TAs' knowledge of the curriculum and the course/programme requirements are inadequate, and the level of challenge is often wrongly pitched; low demands are placed on learners by teachers and TAs. • The methods used by teachers and TAs do not sufficiently engage and encourage the learners. • Not enough independent learning takes place and/or learners are excessively passive. • Assessment is not frequent or accurate enough to monitor learners' progress, resulting in teachers and TAs not having a clear enough understanding of learners' needs. • Learners do not know how to improve. • There is inadequate use of resources, including teaching assistants and time available. • Teaching assistants and parents/carers are inadequately guided and helped to support learners. • There are a limited range of enrichment activities and extended services, and opportunities for learners to take responsibility in the community. • Learners do not engage readily with the community.

Source: adapted from Ofsted 2006g: 11–12.

Table 7.4 Evaluating *Every Child Matters* outcomes

ECM outcomes	Ofsted judgement criteria and evidence descriptors for *Every Child Matters* outcomes			
	Outstanding (1)	Good (2)	Satisfactory (3)	Inadequate (4)
Be healthy	Developing healthy lifestyles is a high priority. Very good provision for and participation in physical activities. Health education/PSHE valued and believed in by pupils. Very good opportunities exist for healthy eating and drinking. High levels of care alert staff to learners with problems and these are dealt with adeptly. Learners make very good progress in learning to recognise stress. School's support for learners in trouble is very good. Pupils' self-esteem is very good.	Majority of learners undertake 5 hours of organised PE, sport per week. School has well-organised and well-received health, drugs and sex education programmes. Good facilities exist on site for eating and drinking healthily. Lunches offer a balanced diet and vending machines contain healthy options. Staff are alert to the well-being of learners. Learners make good progress in recognising and dealing with stress and feel they can easily get support from staff when needed.	Great majority of learners undertake at least 5 hours of PE/sport per week. School has in place a satisfactory programme for health education, including drugs and sex education. Facilities exist for learners to eat and drink healthily on site. Learners are taught to recognise symptoms relating to a lack of mental well-being and have access to support when needed. Staff have adequate support to enable them to recognise health problems and refer them appropriately.	The curriculum and facilities do not adequately promote a healthy life style. A significant number of learners don't have 5 hours of organised PE/sport per week. Health education provision, including that for drugs and sex, are deficient in range. Adequate facilities do not exist for learners to eat and drink healthily on site, or they are not encouraged sufficiently to do so. Distressed learners do not have their needs adequately supported. Learners self-esteem is very low.
Stay safe	Safety of learners is a very high priority. Risk assessments make learning activities safe. Learners feel very safe and know that they are very well supported when threatened by any form of intimidation. Learners undertake all physical activities in a very orderly and sensible manner. Learners have a very good understanding of how to manage risk in their own lives. Learners have a very good sense of their own and others' safety at school and in its immediate surroundings. Learners adopt very safe practices in lessons like science and technology.	Good all-round approach to ensuring learners' stay safe. Child protection procedures are clear and effective. Risk assessments are thorough and result in effective action. Learners feel safe. Learners make good use of systems to report bullying, racism and harassment and staff act decisively to protect them. Learners are taught to play sports safely.	Reasonable steps are taken to ensure safety of all learners. Child protection arrangements are in place. Staff undertake adequate risk assessments and act effectively upon them, making sure that dangerous materials and medicines are secure. Learners feel safe, and know and make use of reporting system for bullying. Learners are taught to swim.	Adequate steps are not taken to ensure that learners are safe. There is a lack of adequate child protection arrangements. Learners are exposed to unacceptable risks, resulting from inadequate risk assessment. Reporting systems for bullying, racism and harassment are ineffective. Learners report they don't feel safe.

Table 7.4 (Continued)

ECM outcomes	Ofsted judgement criteria and evidence descriptors for *Every Child Matters* outcomes			
	Outstanding (1)	Good (2)	Satisfactory (3)	Inadequate (4)
Enjoy and achieve	Standards are rising very fast or being maintained at very high levels. Virtually all learners make very good progress and enjoy learning very much. Personal development is very good, as shown in learners' high self-esteem, high aspirations and increasing independence. High quality provision and teaching exist. Different groups of learners' punctuality and attendance at school is very good.	Standards are rising fast and compare well with similar schools. Learners make good progress and no significant groups lag behind. Learners enjoy their education a great deal and have positive attitudes and good behaviour. Learners make good progress in their personal qualities. Provision and teaching are of good quality. Strengths and weaknesses are known and also what must be done to improve.	Standards are rising steadily and are broadly in line with those in similar schools. Most learners make at least satisfactory progress in the majority of subjects, courses and areas of learning. No group of learners underachieves significantly. Learners generally enjoy their learning as shown by their satisfactory attitudes, behaviour and attendance. The personal development of most learners is satisfactory. The teaching, curriculum, recreational activities and monitoring of progress are satisfactory overall. Groups in difficulty are identified and there are adequate strategies to assist them.	Significant numbers of learners do not enjoy their education and/or do not achieve adequately. The quality of provision or the effectiveness of management are inadequate to make the outcomes satisfactory. Significant number of learners display disaffection. There are marked deficiencies in one or more aspects of learners' personal development. Provision and teaching are unsatisfactory. There is a lack of accurate self-evaluation and ineffective action arising from this. Punctuality and attendance at school among different groups of learners is unsatisfactory.
Make a positive contribution	Learners make a very strong contribution to the community. Learners are taught about their rights and encouraged and empowered to express their views very effectively. There is a self-disciplined community in which bullying and discrimination is very rare, and when it occurs is dealt with most effectively.	Learners make a good contribution to the community. They have a clear understanding of their rights, a confidence to express their views and form constructive relationships with adults. Bullying and discrimination are rare and are dealt with effectively. Learners' views are listened to and they are actively involved in.	Learners have a satisfactory understanding of their rights and a reasonable understanding of how to bring about change. The incidence of bullying and discrimination is not high. Learners express their points of view, and several activities are initiated and managed by them. Adequate steps are taken to listen to the views of learners, help them.	Learners don't make an adequate contribution to their community and are not sufficiently encouraged to do so. Learners have an inadequate understanding of their rights and participation in decisions that affect them. There is extensive bullying and discrimination. There is a low level of learner involvement in communal activities.

Table 7.4 (Continued)

ECM outcomes	Ofsted judgement criteria and evidence descriptors for *Every Child Matters* outcomes			
	Outstanding (1)	Good (2)	Satisfactory (3)	Inadequate (4)
	Learners' views are central to the decisions made by the school. Learners have a very high level of involvement in community activities. Citizenship is a very strong part of the taught curriculum and in the life of the learners. Learners relate very well to each other and to adults, and build positive relationships with people from different backgrounds.	Activities that affect the community. Citizenship is well embedded in the curriculum.	To form positive relationships with adults, and take on responsibility. Clear policies exist to combat bullying and harassment, action is taken to reduce incidents of them and victims have good access to support.	Significant shortfalls exist in the citizenship curriculum. There are inadequate mechanisms and action to deal with bullying and harassment.
Achieve economic well-being	High priority is given to developing the self-confidence skills of learners. Challenging teaching styles and a wide range of engaging and demanding activities enable learners to make very good progress in their capacity to handle change and take initiative. Learners make confident strides in their financial literacy. The area of economic well-being is most carefully monitored and imaginatively developed.	Learners make good progress in acquiring the skills and qualities that will enable them to do well at work. The teaching styles and available activities effectively promote enterprising qualities in learners. Financial literacy is a strong part of the curriculum and learners progress well. The provision for this area of the curriculum is carefully monitored and continuously improved.	Learners acquire, as appropriate for their age, the skills and personal qualities that will enable them to succeed at work. A range of teaching styles and enrichment opportunities satisfactorily promote these skills and qualities. Learners make satisfactory progress in their financial literacy. The quality of work-related learning is reviewed accurately and adequate action is taken to remedy any weaknesses.	Learners don't make adequate progress in the skills and personal qualities that will enable them to succeed at work. There is slow progress made in acquiring work-related skills. Teaching styles are overly didactic and don't enable learners to develop their personal qualities and skills, or their enterprise capability. Major gaps exist in provision – particularly at KS4.

Source: adapted from Ofsted 2006g: 9–10.

1 Characteristics of the school – main characteristics; distinctive aims; any special features; any aids to achievement; contextual issues that may create barriers to raising performance; main priorities in the school improvement plan.

2 Views of learners, parents/carers and other stakeholders – about the learners' standards, personal development and well-being and the quality of provision; actions taken based on views of learners, parents/carers and other stakeholders; effectiveness of actions taken.

3 Achievement and standards – how well learners achieve; standards in their work; the attainment and progress of different groups of pupils.

4 Personal development and well-being – how good is the overall personal development and well-being of the learners (ECM outcomes); to what extent learners adopt healthy lifestyles; to what extent learners feel safe and adopt safe practices; how much learners enjoy their education; how well learners make a positive contribution to the community; how well learners prepare for their future economic well-being.

5 The quality of provision – how good and effective is the quality of teaching and learning; how well does the curriculum and other activities meet the needs and interests of learners; how well learners are guided and supported.

6 Leadership and management – impact on the outcomes for learners and the quality of provision; overall effectiveness and efficiency of leadership and management in raising achievement and supporting all learners.

7 Overall effectiveness – how effective and efficient is the provision of education, and any integrated care, extended services in meeting the needs of learners including its main strengths and weaknesses; what the effectiveness of any steps taken to promote improvement since the last inspection, and as a result of the school's self-evaluation; what the capacity is to make further improvement; how effective links are with other organisations to promote the well-being of learners, and, what steps need to be taken to improve the provision further.

The SEF also expects schools to:

- set out the main evidence on which their evaluation is based;
- identify strengths and weaknesses;
- explain the actions the school is taking to remedy any weaknesses and develop the strengths.

The SEF takes into account the requirement of the *Every Child Matters* five outcomes and the related Children Act 2004, largely in Part A, section 4.

TAs will provide valuable evidence to all sections of Part A of the SEF and in particular to:

- section 3 – TAs contributions to learners' achievement and standards;
- section 4 – TAs contributions to learners' personal development and well-being;
- section 5 – TAs contributions to the quality of provision in guiding and supporting learners;
- section 6 – the leadership and management of TA deployment.

PUPIL SURVEY ON TEACHING ASSISTANT SUPPORT

Introduction
Thank you for agreeing to complete this survey.
Your responses are confidential and anonymous.
Please answer each question fully and honestly.
(Well-being refers to you feeling happy, safe, healthy, valued and respected, able to cope with change, and to work with and help others in school and in the local community)

Year Group/Class: ....   **Date:** ....

Questions

1. When do you find support for learning and well-being from teaching assistants is most useful?

2. How do you prefer to receive support for learning and well-being from teaching assistants?

3. Do you like having the same teaching assistant all the time or different teaching assistants to support your learning and well-being? Give a reason for your answer.

4. How else could teaching assistants support pupils' learning and well-being in school?

5. How could pupils have more of a say about the type of support for learning and well-being they get from teaching assistants?

6. What else could teaching assistants do to help pupils make decisions, become more self-confident, and manage change in their lives?

7. When do you find support from teaching assistants least helpful?

8. What else could the school do to make teaching assistant support for pupils' learning and well-being even better?

9. Is there anything else you would like to comment on about teaching assistant support for pupils in school?

Please post your completed survey in the post box in the school's main entrance.

Figure 7.1 Seeking the views of learners about teaching assistant support.

Guidance for TAs on the type of evidence to contribute to the school's SEF

When completing the SEF, TAs together need to:

- jot down the most important points to include in response to the relevant Ofsted SEF questions and prompts – keep these brief and to the point, and jargon-free;
- ensure evidence is accurate and evaluative not descriptive, and relates to impact on outcomes for pupils, as Ofsted will cross-check this during inspection;

Table 7.5 The self-evaluation form – Part A

SEF aspect	Impact of TA support/ learners' outcomes	Evidence source	TA support – strengths and weaknesses	Action taken to improve	Action required – areas for further improvement
1. SCHOOL CHARACTERISTICS (a) Main characteristics of the learners you support					
(b) Any distinctive aims or special features of the school that you contribute to as a TA, e.g. extended school activities, special unit provision					
(c) Any specific contextual issues acting as aids or barriers to raising pupil performance in your TA support role					
(d) Any additional school characteristics that relate to your TA support role, e.g. IIP, ECO, Healthy Schools, Awards, Arts Mark or Sports Mark Awards					
(e) Brief outline of the main priorities for TAs (on the development plan), and how they reflect the context in which you work					
2. VIEWS OF LEARNERS, PARENTS/CARERS AND OTHER STAKEHOLDERS (a) How do you gather the views of learners, parents/carers and other stakeholders about your TA support?					

Table 7.5 (*Continued*)

SEF aspect	Impact of TA support/ learners' outcomes	Evidence source	TA support – strengths and weaknesses	Action taken to improve	Action required – areas for further improvement
(b) What do those views tell you about learners' achievements, standards, personal development and well-being, in relation to the quality of your TA support?					
(c) How do you share these findings about their views with parents/ carers and other stakeholders?					
(d) Action taken based on the views of parents/carers and other stakeholders, with an evaluation of the effectiveness of what you did as a TA supporting learners					
3. ACHIEVEMENT AND STANDARDS (How well learners achieve as a result of TA support) (a) What are the learners' TAs support, achievements and standards of work?					
(b) Where relevant, how well do learners achieve in the Foundation Stage as a result of TA support? Or: How well do learners achieve in the sixth form as a result of TA support?					
(c) On the basis of your evaluation, what are TAs' key priorities for development in relation to this aspect?					
Overall, how well learners achieve as a result of TA support				Ofsted GRADE (1–4):	

Table 7.5 (Continued)

SEF aspect	Impact of TA support/ learners' outcomes	Evidence source	TA support – strengths and weaknesses	Action taken to improve	Action required – areas for further improvement
4. PERSONAL DEVELOPMENT AND WELL-BEING (a) To what extent do learners' TAs support adopt healthy lifestyles?					
(b) To what extent do the learners' TAs support feel safe and adopt safe practices, e.g. safe use of ICT, safe from bullying					
(c) How much do the learners' TAs support enjoy their education? e.g. SMSC attitudes, behaviour, attendance and participation					
(d) How well do the learners TAs support make a positive contribution in class, to the school, and to the wider community? e.g. voice and choice					
(e) How well do the learners TAs support prepare for their future economic well-being? e.g. enterprise and financial capability; literacy, numeracy and ICT					
(f) Where relevant, how good are the learners' personal development and well-being TAs support in the Foundation Stage? OR:					
How good are the learners personal development and well-being, TAs support in the sixth form?					
(g) On the basis of your evaluation, what are the key priorities for development in this aspect?					

Overall progress of the learners supported by TAs in personal development and well-being

Ofsted GRADE (1–4):

Table 7.5 *(Continued)*

SEF aspect	Impact of TA support/ learners' outcomes	Evidence source	TA support – strengths and weaknesses	Action taken to improve	Action required – areas for further improvement
5. THE QUALITY OF PROVISION (a) How good is the quality and impact of TA support for teaching and learning, and for behaviour management?					
(b) How well do the curriculum/extra curricula activities and other support/interventions TAs offer meet learners' needs, interests and ECM outcomes?					
(c) How well are learners guided and supported by TAs? e.g. reduce absence; integrate learners back into mainstream; safeguard learners welfare.					
(d) Where relevant, how good is the quality of TA support provision and day care in the Foundation Stage? Or:					
How good is the quality of TA support provided in the sixth form?					
(e) On the basis of your evaluation, what are TAs key priorities for development in this aspect?					
Overall quality of TA support for teaching and learning in the classes/subjects supported					Ofsted GRADE (1–4):
Overall quality of curriculum/extra curricular activities and other TA support/interventions offered					Ofsted GRADE (1–4):
Overall quality of the care, guidance and support TAs offer to learners					Ofsted GRADE (1–4):

Table 7.5 (*Continued*)

SEF aspect	Impact of TA support/ learners' outcomes	Evidence source	TA support – strengths and weaknesses	Action taken to improve	Action required – areas for further improvement
6. LEADERSHIP AND MANAGEMENT (of TA deployment) (a) What is the overall effectiveness of leadership and management of TA support and deployment? e.g. TA performance management; impact of TA CPD on the learners' outcomes					
(b) Where relevant: What is the effectiveness of leadership and management of TA support and deployment in the Foundation Stage? Or: What is the effectiveness and efficiency of leadership and management of TA support and deployment in the sixth form?					
(c) On the basis of your evaluation, what are TAs key priorities for development in this aspect?					
Overall effectiveness and efficiency of the leadership and management of TA support and deployment					Ofsted GRADE (1–4):

Table 7.5 (Continued)

SEF aspect	Impact of TA support/ learners' outcomes	Evidence source	TA support – strengths and weaknesses	Action taken to improve	Action required – areas for further improvement
7. OVERALL EFFECTIVENESS AND EFFICIENCY (a) What is the overall effectiveness of provision, including any extended services, delivered by TAs, and its main strengths and weaknesses?					
(b) What is the effectiveness of any steps taken to promote improvement in TA support and deployment since the last inspection?					
(c) What is the capacity to make further improvement in TA support and deployment to meet the personalised learning and ECM agendas?					
(d) What steps need to be taken to improve TA support and provision further?					
(e) Where relevant: What are the overall quality and standards of TA provision in the Foundation Stage? Or:					
(f) What is the effectiveness and efficiency of TA provision overall in the sixth form?					
Overall effectiveness of TA provision (whole school)				Ofsted GRADE (1–4):	
Capacity to make further improvement in TA support, provision and deployment				Ofsted GRADE (1–4):	
Improvement in TA provision since the last inspection				Ofsted GRADE (1–4):	
Effectiveness and efficiency of TA provision in the Foundation Stage				Ofsted GRADE (1–4):	
Effectiveness and efficiency of TA provision in the sixth form				Ofsted GRADE (1–4):	

Source: adapted from Ofsted 2005c.

- avoid repetition in SEF evidence – cross-reference where appropriate;
- begin by completing section 3 (achievement and standards) and section 4 (personal development and well-being) of the SEF first;
- when judging the quality of TA support against Ofsted grades and criteria, be sure to link this to impact on pupils' outcomes.

Teaching assistants and Ofsted inspections

The current Ofsted inspection schedule, first introduced in September 2005, places a greater emphasis on:

- school self-evaluation;
- the quality and effectiveness of the school's leadership and management, including governance;
- the impact teaching and support has on pupils' learning, achievements and personal development;
- the well-being of pupils in the light of *Every Child Matters*.

Ofsted base their inspection judgements on the effectiveness of TA support and deployment on a four-point scale:

1 Outstanding: TAs are well directed to support learning. They make a significant contribution in very effectively supporting pupils' learning and well-being. They understand the next steps learners need to take and provide a wide range of learning support activities for learners.
2 Good: TAs are well deployed and are effective in what they do. TAs relate well to learners they support and expect them to work hard.
3 Satisfactory: TAs are utilised adequately. They are not effective in supporting learning because they have an incomplete understanding of expectations, and accept pupils' efforts too readily, without a sufficient level of challenge.
4 Inadequate: TAs are utilised inadequately due to poor management. TAs lack the necessary knowledge, skills and understanding, thus contributing little to lessons, pupils' learning and well-being.

Ofsted inspectors will gather a wide range of telling evidence in order to judge the effectiveness of TA deployment, as well as the impact of their support on pupils' learning and well-being outcomes. This evidence includes:

- TA contributions to the school's SEF;
- snapshots of lesson observations where TAs are supporting pupils;
- scrutiny of teacher planning, TA records of pupil support, whole school provision map for inclusion/ECM;
- sampling of pupils' work and achievements;
- data analysis of pupils' learning and ECM well-being outcomes;
- focused discussions with members of the school leadership team, the Inclusion Manager, SENCO, governors, parents/carers, pupils and TA representatives from the school Learning and Well-being Team to clarify TA role and deployment.

The Ofsted inspection schedule for schools covers the same areas as those in the SEF, but in a different order:

Ofsted inspection schedule for schools

Overall effectiveness
How effective and efficient are the provision and related services in meeting the full range of learners' needs and why?

Achievement and Standards
1   How well do learners achieve?

Quality of Provision
2   How effective are teaching, training and learning?
3   How well do programmes and activities meet the needs and interests of learners?
4   How well are learners guided and supported?

Leadership and Management
5   How effective are leadership and management in raising achievement and supporting all learners?

(Ofsted 2005a: 18–20)

Teaching assistants preparing for the school Ofsted inspection

TAs need to be very clear about the impact their contributions make to the relevant evaluation requirements for each aspect of the inspection schedule, and where appropriate, its alignment with the five *Every Child Matters* (ECM) outcomes. Table 7.6 provides a useful overview of the Ofsted inspection requirements. This will enable TAs to know, and be better prepared for, the range of evidence inspectors will gather prior to and during the inspection.

Further activities for teaching assistants

The following questions on aspects covered in this chapter are designed to promote further discussion and help to identify ways forward in enabling TAs to effectively monitor and evaluate the impact of their pupil support in meeting the *Every Child Matters* outcomes.

- How do you gather evidence to demonstrate that the pupils you support are making sufficient progress towards meeting the five ECM outcomes?
- If a pupil you support is not achieving successfully on any of the ECM outcomes, what else could you do to help them improve in these?
- How do you intend to monitor and evaluate the impact of your support in relation to improving the ECM outcomes for the pupils you work with?
- How do you feed back evidence of the impact of your support work to inform the school's self-evaluation form (SEF)?
- How do you feedback to class/subject teachers and any other paraprofessionals on the effectiveness of your support, in improving learning and ECM well-being outcomes for pupils they teach or work with?
- How do you utilise and act on the information you receive from teachers, other colleagues and external professionals on improving outcomes for pupils?
- How far does TA support in your school lead to sustained pupil improvement and progress in learning and ECM well-being?
- To what extent are the teachers you support and work alongside, accountable for the effectiveness and impact of your support with pupils?

Table 7.6 Ofsted inspection requirements with examples of evidence of TA impact

Inspection aspect and evaluation requirements	Example of TA evidence of impact
Overall effectiveness: • Overall effectiveness of TA provision, including extended services, and its main strengths and weaknesses	Annual parents/carers, pupils, staff surveys indicate positive comments in relation to the value and effectiveness of TA support. TAs have increased LAC and vulnerable pupils' motivation and attitude to learning by 75 per cent. Teacher absence rates have fallen considerably since TA support has been increased in classrooms. The school has a good reputation for the quality of its TA support, and the LA frequently send new TAs from other schools to observe best TA practice. After-school clubs delivered by TAs as part of extended school service provision are oversubscribed. A potential weakness is how to sustain and retain the current number of TAs in the future, when the school is beginning to experience falling rolls.
• The capacity to make further improvements in TA support and deployment • The effectiveness of any steps taken to promote improvement in TA support and deployment since the last inspection	The formation of the school Personalised Learning and Well-being Team, of which TAs are key members, offers the future opportunity for TAs to support and work with more able, gifted and talented pupils by supporting enrichment opportunities, i.e. art club, puzzle club, chess club. Workforce remodelling and single status agreement has enabled TA job descriptions to be reviewed and updated in line with the NOS for supporting teaching and learning in the classroom and the Every Child Matters agenda. The impact of this staffing restructuring has entailed TAs strengths, talents, interests and aptitudes to be maximised upon, leading to more effective deployment across the school. The school's CPD programme for TAs has been broadened to include specific training on aspects of personalised learning and Every Child Matters, which has improved the effectiveness of their support for pupils' learning and well-being in the classroom.
• Where appropriate, the effectiveness of links with other organisations to enable TAs to promote the well-being of learners	Termly pupil review meetings are held by the members of the Personalised learning and well-being team which includes contributions from TAs and front-line workers from external agencies who support and work with pupils in school. This has strengthened collaborative partnership working and enhanced greater information sharing about pupils' progress and achievements in learning and well-being. TAs have each been assigned to one of the five ECM outcomes and they make valuable contributions to helping the ECM Focus Group in school further develop and enhance personalised learning and well-being outcomes for pupils. A senior TA who has just achieved HLTA status takes responsibility for cross-phase transfer links with partner schools for pupils with additional needs. This ensures continuity in personalised learning and well-being provision carries on in the next phase of education.

Table 7.6 *(Continued)*

Inspection aspect and evaluation requirements	Example of TA evidence of impact
• The quality of standards of TA support and deployment in the Foundation Stage	The recent Ofsted inspection identified TA support in the FS as being outstanding. This continues to add considerable value to children's achievements in all aspects of the FS curriculum. Early high quality support for children's learning and personal development has resulted in fewer children identified as having SEN, on transfer to KS1.
• The effectiveness and efficiency of any TA support in the Sixth Form	TA support in the sixth form takes the form of Access Facilitator who develops LDD students' independent learning and study skills. The TA provides support and advice on the use of ICT and other technological and specialist aids to promote and enhance flexible learning and individual study at home and school. The assigned TA also provides quality assurance checks on college and work-related learning placements for LDD students.
Achievement and Standards: 1. How well do learners achieve as a result of TA support?	Barriers to learning and participation are quickly identified, minimised and removed by TAs, working in partnership with teachers and other paraprofessionals on the Personalised Learning and Well-being Team. This has resulted in enhanced curriculum and extra-curricular access for those pupils with additional needs and from vulnerable groups. Learners are able to achieve their optimum potential as a result of appropriately targeted TA support and personalised intervention programmes for learning and well-being. In most cases pupils supported catch up with and in some instances exceed the progress of their peers. Teachers' report that TAs keep pupils on task, increase learner motivation and self confidence. PASS findings also support this evidence.
• Learners' success in achieving challenging targets/learning goals	TAs in partnership with teachers and learners agree upon challenging and realistic class and individual pupil targets being set for learning and ECM well-being. The improved system for TA tracking and monitoring pupil progress has resulted in more sharply focused evidence of the impact of TA support on pupil outcomes. 95 per cent of learners receiving additional TA support have met their set targets. This is a 35 per cent increase on the previous year, and continues to improve.
• The standards of learners' work in relation to their learning goals	Standards of learners' work in relation to learning goals set are continuing to improve in the FS and in KS1 and 2. This is as a result of TAs targeting and focusing their support more appropriately to meet the personalised learning needs of pupils. Evaluation of the intervention programmes delivered by TAs in speech and language, phonics and writing clearly indicate a marked improvement of standards in these particular aspects.
• Learners' progress relative to their prior attainment and potential	TA pupil tracking sheets for personalised learning and ECM outcomes clearly demonstrate good value added progress as a result of their support and interventions, which has enabled all pupils supported to improve in relation to their starting points.

Table 7.6 (*Continued*)

Inspection aspect and evaluation requirements	Example of TA evidence of impact
• The extent to which learners enjoy their work with TAs	Verbal feedback to teachers and findings from the learners' annual survey on the extent to which they enjoy their work with TAs indicates a 100 per cent satisfaction level. Evaluations from lunch time and after-school clubs run by TAs are positive and record high levels of pupil enjoyment in participating in these activities.
• The emotional development of learners	The whole school INSET on emotional intelligence has enabled TAs along with teachers and non-teaching staff to gain a better understanding of pupils' emotional well-being needs and to ensure they provide a secure and safe emotionally intelligent learning environment. The annual pupil survey indicates that the majority of learners feel able to trust supporting adults to help them manage their feelings and emotions. TAs are delivering elements of the SEAL programme, which is already showing a marked improvement in pupils developing good levels of emotional intelligence.
• The behaviour of learners	TAs ongoing CPD on managing pupils' behaviour is already demonstrating an improvement in pupil behaviour during lessons and at break and lunchtimes. Fewer children are being sent by TAs to class teachers and/or to the headteacher/deputy headteacher due to TAs employing effective consistent behaviour management strategies.
• The attendance of learners	TAs are taking into account the attendance of pupils being supported when they are tracking and monitoring the rates of pupils' progress in personalised learning and ECM outcomes. TAs are rewarding pupils for improved attendance at support and intervention sessions, and data analysis already indicates attendance rates of pupils have improved by over 60 per cent on the previous year.
• The extent to which learners adopt safe practices and a healthy lifestyle	TAs contributions to supporting and promoting the 'Stay Safe Live Longer' initiative, in partnership with external partners such as the police, sports coach, school nurse have considerably helped to increase pupils' awareness of the importance of following healthy lifestyles and safe practices in school, at home and in the wider community.
• Learners' spiritual, moral, social and cultural development	Evaluations of TAs supporting the delivery of SEAL and PSHE programmes indicate an improvement in pupils respecting, understanding and tolerating others values, beliefs and cultural diversity. Observations of TAs in-class have found TAs enabling pupils to make responsible and reasoned judgements and decisions on moral dilemmas, knowing right from wrong, and asking questions to improve their understanding of global and real life issues. TAs delivering programmes on restorative justice, conflict resolution and social skills to targeted pupils has helped to enable those learners to take on responsibilities, develop positive relationships with peers and adults and to become more effective and cooperative learners.

Table 7.6 (*Continued*)

Inspection aspect and evaluation requirements	Example of TA evidence of impact
• Whether learners make a positive contribution to the community	TAs have been reported by teachers to provide sensitive and discrete support for pupils when they are undertaking projects that engage them in wider community participation. This support has contributed to increasing pupils' confidence, self-esteem and independence. Local residents have praised the work of the school's ECO Recycling Group and also the Wildlife Garden Development Team for improving the local surrounding area near to the school.
The Quality of Provision: 2. How effective are teaching, training and learning? • How well teaching and/or training and resources (including support for learning) promote learning, address the full range of learners' needs and meet course/programme requirements	TA/teacher partnership working has strengthened through the embedding of the Leading on Intervention strategy and the formation of the Personalised Learning and Well-being Team in school. This has resulted in qualitative and quantitative data from TA and teacher tracking and recording of pupil progress in learning and well-being better informing personalised learning approaches, curriculum delivery, targeted TA support and intervention programmes which are tailored and more responsive to learners' needs. Already there has been a steady upward trend in the results at the end of KS1 and KS2.
• The suitability and rigour of assessment in planning and monitoring learners' progress	The whole school INSET on assessment for learning has enabled teachers and TAs to engage pupils more proactively in reviewing and self-assessing their own progress and provision in learning and well-being. This has also helped to sharpen the focus of teaching, learning and support to focus on the impact of outcomes for learners. TAs becoming involved in the moderation of pupils' work and achievements with class teachers has helped to improve the tailoring of their support and interventions for pupils with additional needs. It has also ensured that valid and consistent judgements about pupil attainment, progress and achievements are made whole school. The introduction of the termly Pupil Progress Meetings throughout the school, has helped to engage those from external agencies, TAs and teachers to have a high quality dialogue focused on improving outcomes for children and evaluating the impact of teaching, interventions, support and wrap-around care more closely. Improved quality of formative and summative assessment information and data analysis has helped to improve the quality of target setting, target acquisition and personalised learning and personalised service provision for pupils.
• The identification of, and provision for, additional learning needs	Enhanced collaborative teamwork between teachers, TAs and external front-line workers from health, social care and education has improved the earlier identification of underachieving, vulnerable and LDD pupils. Targeted support and interventions have been put in place earlier, and this has resulted in fewer children being identified at action and action plus on the SEN register, as their needs are fully met within the inclusive classroom, at Wave 1 'quality first teaching'. TAs and teachers feel more confident and competent in meeting the needs of pupils with additional needs.

Table 7.6 (Continued)

Inspection aspect and evaluation requirements	Example of TA evidence of impact
• The involvement of parents and carers in their children's learning and development	Some TAs are engaged with the Personalised Learning Manager and relevant subject leaders in delivering the Family Learning Sessions and Parent/Carer Workshops on enabling parents/carers to support their child's learning and behaviour at home. These activities have been well attended, and TAs have helped to minimise parents/carers anxieties about supporting their own child's learning in literacy, numeracy and behaviour at home.
3. How well do programmes and activities meet the needs and interests of learners? • The extent to which programmes or activities match learners' aspirations and potential, building on prior attainment and experience	Evaluations on TA support from teachers, pupils and parents/carers, and TAs themselves indicate 100 per cent satisfaction levels in the appropriateness of support activities and interventions in removing barriers to learning and enhancing curriculum access. Stakeholders consider TAs, along with teachers and other paraprofessionals, are enabling learners to reach their optimum potential. The pupil level data for learning and well-being indicates that personalised learning and personalised services are tailored and far more responsive to learners' needs. TAs have built up a secure evidence base as to which support strategies and intervention/catch-up programmes are most effective, and give the highest and quickest impact. TAs and teachers are sensitive to pupils' aspirations, potential and interests and wherever possible, ensure that the curriculum and support activities reflect learners' interests. Improved pupil level data tracking and analysis by TAs and teachers has helped to raise expectations and already demonstrates good value added progress in pupils' learning and well-being outcomes. TAs and teachers in their teaching and support ensure that they utilise a range of multi-sensory and accelerated learning approaches with pupils.
• How far programmes or the curriculum meet external requirements and are responsive to local circumstances	TAs knowledge of the local community has enhanced links with local businesses and voluntary/community organisations. This has begun to enrich and enhance the curriculum/extra curricular provision for pupils through local businesses and organisations sponsoring and supporting curriculum initiatives by sharing their expertise, resources and facilities. TAs, along with teachers, have continued to support pupils in making positive contributions to the community. For example, two TAs have been leading the 'Go Green' recycling project and the development of the Wild Life Garden on a piece of waste land adjacent to the school. Members of the local community have expressed their appreciation of pupils helping to improve their local environment.
• The extent to which enrichment activities and/or extended services contribute to learners' enjoyment and achievement	Oral feedback from pupils to teachers, parents/carers, as well as comments on the annual pupil survey indicates that they greatly enjoy the enrichment activities and extended school provision they have attended, some of which has been delivered and supported by TAs. The pupils felt that these activities had helped them to achieve more self-confidence, make new friends and learn new skills.

Table 7.6 (*Continued*)

Inspection aspect and evaluation requirements	Example of TA evidence of impact
• The extent to which the provision contributes to the learners' capacity to stay safe and healthy	TAs organise and operate the 'Walking Bus' to and from school scheme. The impact of this has been a reduction in the number of pupils travelling to and from school in parents'/carers' cars. TAs act as positive role models to pupils in eating and drinking healthily and enjoying exercise during the school day, leading the popular 'walking the golden mile' playground activity with pupils. TAs undertake risk assessments when they are working with and supporting pupils on outdoor and environmental activities, and no pupils' safety has been compromised.
4. How well are learners guided and supported? • The care, advice, guidance and other support provided to safeguard welfare, promote personal development and achieve high standards	All TAs have received training in child protection procedures and safeguarding children. While TAs respect pupil confidentiality, training has increased TA awareness to report any concerns about pupil welfare immediately to the named child protection officer in school. Lesson observations of TAs supporting pupils, indicates that learners have formed trusting relationships with supporting adults. TAs ensure that the pupils they are supporting work in a safe and healthy environment, conducive to learning. TAs support the induction of new pupils into the school by tracking and monitoring these children's emotional, social and personal development and well-being. This system has already begun to reduce the anxiety levels of new pupils who report they find the TA care and support invaluable to making them feel more confident. TAs organise and run the pupil 'Befriending' scheme, which involves them in training pupils to act as playground buddies and study buddies to new and lonely children. The impact of this scheme has been 100 per cent successful in making new and isolated children feel included, welcomed and valued as a member of the school community.
• The quality and accessibility of information, advice and guidance to learners in relation to courses and programmes, and, where applicable, career progression	Due to the TA's knowledge of which intervention programmes are most effective and give high impact and a quick return for learners, the learning gap is closing for those pupils who are vulnerable or at risk of underachieving. TAs are 'Champions for Children' and comments from pupils on the annual survey indicate that pupils consider TAs to help them become more confident, to feel better about themselves, and help them to overcome difficulties with learning. TAs have proved to be a valuable conduit for signposting pupils who need further advice and guidance about school work or personal issues to other key staff on the Personalised Learning and Well-being Team.
Leadership and Management: 5. How effective are leadership and management in raising achievement and supporting all learners? • How effectively performance is monitored and improved through quality assurance and self-assessment	The annual individual appraisal and development meeting for all TAs has helped to identify strengths and areas for further development to increase the effectiveness of TA support and interventions. TAs record in their portfolio of professional development the impact any in-house and external training they have attended has had on helping them to improve pupils' learning and well-being outcomes. Recent external accreditation through the acquisition of Investors in People, the Basic Skills Quality Mark and the Inclusion Quality Mark have involved TAs as key stakeholders in contributing evidence to support quality assurance procedures in improving outcomes for children.

Table 7.6 (Continued)

Inspection aspect and evaluation requirements	Example of TA evidence of impact
• The adequacy and suitability of specialist equipment, learning resources and accommodation	The school is fortunate to be well resourced with specialist equipment, high quality and up-to-date learning resources, which includes: a good supply of ICT hardware and software within classrooms, spacious and flexible modern purpose-built accommodation to enable pupils to study independently, learn within small groups and as a whole class. All TAs have had training in the use of ICT, which includes the use of PowerPoint, digital cameras, interactive white boards and PDAs, and their proficiency in its use and application has enhanced the quality of learning support for pupils of all abilities. TAs are fortunate to be able to work from and within a state-of-the-art Learning Resource Base which is where they can produce tailored and customised curriculum resources, undertake smaller group interventions with pupils, undertake training and administrative tasks. TAs in their annual appraisal and survey have indicated that this enhanced working environment has improved the quality of their support and intervention work. The school has developed a Well-being Centre which is a shared resource between a cluster of three local schools, where teaching and non-teaching staff, parents/carers, pupils can receive therapeutic interventions, such as aromatherapy, reflexology, head, hand and foot massage and relaxation techniques. The emotional well-being of staff and pupils has improved greatly, resulting in a decrease in staff absence and more pupils being calm, relaxed and able to manage their feelings and anger more effectively.
• How effectively and efficiently resources are deployed to achieve value for money	The deployment of resources, which includes TA support, has been greatly improved through the introduction of provision management and provision mapping for inclusion and ECM to meet pupils' additional needs. The ECM inclusion whole school provision map is kept under regular review. An annual audit to identify additional provision, and which interventions and programmes of support have worked best in improving learning and well-being outcomes for pupils takes place. TAs make significant and valuable contributions to the collection of qualitative and quantitative evidence for this process.
• How effective are links made with other providers, services, employers and other organisations to promote the integration of care, education and any extended services to enhance learning and to promote well-being and community cohesion	The formation of the school Personalised Learning and Well-being Team has promoted closer partnership working between teachers, TAs, front-line workers from external agencies, voluntary and community organisations and partners. There is a common shared understanding and clarity of respective roles that focus on removing barriers to learning and participation, and improving learning and ECM well-being outcomes for children, and joint INSET. TAs have been empowered and supported to develop new skills and talents in areas such as pupil counselling, and anger management. They clearly see the link between learning and well-being. The production of information leaflets about the enhanced TA role has helped teachers, parents/carers, pupils and external professionals to understand the role of TAs in supporting personalised learning and ECM well-being.

Table 7.6 (*Continued*)

Inspection aspect and evaluation requirements	Example of TA evidence of impact
• The effectiveness with which governors and other supervisory boards discharge their responsibilities	New members have joined the governing body this year and this has provided an ideal opportunity to review the governors monitoring responsibilities. Five governors each take responsibility for monitoring one of the ECM outcomes. One of these governors is a TA working in the school. Five other governors take responsibility for monitoring one of the aspects of personalised learning. This distributed leadership and management strategy has strengthened governance and enabled them to have a secure view about the school's strengths and weaknesses, and value for money. The impact and effectiveness of TA support and interventions is fed back to the governing body through the curriculum sub-committee meetings, and in the annual report to governors. The HLTA, who is the TA team leader, has given a presentation to the governing body on the success of the cross-phase pupil transfer initiative.

- How far does the feedback given to you as a TA focus on what you do to improve pupils' learning skills, responses, work and achievements?
- In the context of whole school self-evaluation what is distinctive about TA support in your school?
- How good are the learning and well-being outcomes for vulnerable and 'hard-to-reach' pupils in the school, as a result of TA support?

Glossary

Accelerated learning – refers to the range of practical approaches that enable pupils to learn how to learn. It includes utilising approaches such as mind mapping, pole-bridging (talking about the thinking process in learning), multiple intelligences, multi-sensory learning and thinking skills.

Achievement – refers to the pupils' knowledge, skills and understanding gained through the subjects of the curriculum, and the attitudes, values and other aspects of personal development fostered by the school and developed within and beyond the formal curriculum.

Active listening – is a non-judgemental way of listening that focuses entirely on what the pupil is saying and confirms understanding of both the content of the message and the emotions and feelings underlying the message to ensure accurate understanding.

Anaphylaxis – is an acute, severe allergic reaction requiring immediate medical attention, which occurs within seconds or minutes of exposure to a certain food, substance, or the venom of stinging insects like wasps or bees.

Assessment for learning – refers to the process of identifying pupils' learning needs; of seeking and interpreting evidence for use by pupils, teachers and other professionals to decide where the pupils are in their learning, what they need to do to improve and how to get there.

Circle of friends – is an approach to enhancing the inclusion of any pupil who is experiencing difficulties in school as a result of disability, diversity, behaviour or personal crisis, which is making it difficult for them to form friendships. The circle of friends mobilises peers of the pupil concerned to provide support and engage in problem solving with the pupil in difficulty.

Circle time – involves a group of children and young people, working within agreed ground rules, to actively listen to each others concerns, ideas and feelings with mutual respect in a non-judgemental emotionally intelligent environment. It helps to develop positive relationships, creates a sense of belonging, and promotes reflection and solution-focused problem solving.

Coaching – is a structured sustained process of activities which promote and enhance reflective practice and specific aspects of a learner's practice.

Common Assessment Framework – a holistic assessment process used by professionals and practitioners in the children's workforce to assess the additional needs of children and young people at the first signs of difficulties.

Conflict resolution – is the process of attempting to resolve a dispute or conflict amicably. It entails listening to and providing opportunities to meet each party's needs, and adequately addressing their interests in order that they are each satisfied with the outcome. It also involves utilising negotiation, mediation and conciliation skills.

Counselling – refers to a trained professional working alongside pupils in schools, who actively listens to their concerns and difficulties; helps them to explore their own feelings and to learn important things about themselves and their relationships, enables them to reflect on difficult events and who guides them to develop coping strategies and their emotional intelligence.

Cyberbullying – is an aggressive, intentional act carried out by a group or individual, using electronic forms of contact, repeatedly over time against a victim who cannot easily defend him or herself.

Department for Children, Schools and Families (DCSF) – replaced the DfES on 28 June 2007. This department will have a coordinating role on children's health and well-being, their welfare, safety, protection and care, child poverty, 14–19 changes, youth and family policy, the respect agenda and anti-drugs work. It will have responsibility for children's social services and schools, as well as preventing youth offending. Along with two other newly created departments: the Department for Innovation, Universities and Skills (DIUS), and the Department for Business, Enterprise and Regulatory Reform (DBERR), it will focus on improving outcomes for children.

Emotional intelligence – refers to the ability to develop emotional sensitivity as well as the capacity to learn healthy emotional management skills.

Emotional literacy – managing own emotions; understanding others' feelings.

Emotional well-being – means having empathy, confidence and self-awareness.

Evaluation – describes the activity where the quality and effectiveness of provision is judged, based on evidence collected by review and monitoring processes.

Extended school – is one that provides a range of services and activities often beyond the school day to help meet the needs of its pupils, their families and the wider community.

Formative assessment – refers to the ongoing assessment at regular intervals of a pupil's progress with accompanying feedback to help them improve their performance.

Gifted – this refers to those pupils who are capable of excelling in one or more academic subjects such as science, history or English.

Inclusion – is concerned with promoting belonging, presence, participation and achievement of the full diversity of children and young people. It is an ongoing process, focused on how children and young people are helped to learn, achieve and participate fully in the activities and life of the school and the community.

Mentoring – refers to the structured sustained process of an experienced adult or older pupil providing mutually agreed activities to support a younger, less experienced pupil, in order to promote and enhance effective transitions, through significant periods of change or challenge in relation to learning or career progression.

Mind mapping – also known as concept mapping or model mapping, it is a useful approach to note-taking, revision, thinking through a problem, or for presenting information to others. Resembling a branch-like structure it has an idea or topic in the centre, with major sub-headings and minor sub-headings or factual information radiating out from it.

Monitoring – is concerned with the systematic regular gathering of information about the extent to which agreed or required plans, policies or statutory requirements are being implemented.

Multiple intelligences – refers to the range of attributes or different intelligences (eight in total, with a possible ninth), that an individual can utilise in the learning process.

Nurture Group – refers to a classroom in a primary or secondary school which provides an informal, domestic, family-like environment for up to 12 children with a teacher and TA, to spend the majority of their school week in, in order to promote and develop their social skills and self-confidence, improve their behaviour and emotional well-being.

Paraprofessional – refers to any individual with the relevant knowledge and skills, who delivers personalised services or who provides additional interventions and support, as part of a multi-disciplinary team, within or across a range of educational settings, which helps to remove barriers to learning.

PASS – this refers to Pupil Attitudes to Self and School which is a rating scale that provides a profile of a pupil's feelings in relation to their self-regard, perceived learning capabilities, perseverance, motivation, general work ethic, attitudes to teachers, their school and attendance, preparedness for learning, confidence in learning, and, response to the curriculum. This profile helps to make the best use of support staff such as TAs, learning mentors and pupil counsellors, and provides a value added measure for the *Every Child Matters* outcomes to inform the school's self evaluation form.

Peer mediation – entails pupils assisting other peers in settling interpersonal conflicts and reaching an agreement in order to enjoy harmonious social relationships. The pupils themselves determine the agreement rather than it being imposed on them by staff in the school, thus ensuring a fair outcome for all involved.

Personalised learning – is the process of tailoring and matching teaching and learning around the way different pupils learn in order to meet their individual needs, interests and aptitudes to enable them to reach their optimum potential.

Personal, Social and Health Education (PSHE) – refers to the planned learning opportunities for pupils in schools aimed at promoting their personal and social development, which includes developing appropriate attitudes, behaviour and values to prepare them for life experiences.

Restorative justice – seeks to restore the relationships between pupils or adults, when these have been damaged by inappropriate or offending behaviour. It is about dialogue, involving others in finding ways forward, mutual respect, negotiating ground rules and building rapport. It utilises skills such as active listening, emotional literacy and anger management.

Review – is a retrospective activity which collects and assesses a wide range of information, which includes perceptions, opinions and judgements relating to a particular programme, initiative or provision. A review process is usually followed by evaluative judgements about the quality of what has been delivered to pupils.

Self-esteem – is a changing and dynamic state. It is about having a good opinion of oneself, feeling worthwhile and liking oneself. Self-esteem is formed when an individual matches up self-image and ideal self. High self-esteem occurs when self-image is good and ideal-self is realistic, and when the individual can cope with failure and is willing to try different things again.

Self-evaluation – is an ongoing, formative, rigorous information gathering process, embedded in the day-to-day work of the classroom and school, which gives an honest assessment of its strengths and weaknesses.

Self-evaluation form (SEF) – is an ongoing summary record of evidence for inspection, and forms only one part of a whole school self-evaluation process.

Social and Emotional Aspects of Learning (SEAL) – covers areas such as self-awareness, managing feelings, motivation, empathy and social skills.

Social stories – are short stories written from a child or young persons perspective, which provide a model for them to emulate and are designed to support their social and emotional development. They help children and young people, particularly those with ASD or ADHD, to adapt to social situations, develop empathy, help them to understand others views, and to interpret daily events appropriately.

Spiritual, moral, social and cultural development (SMSC) – is about preparing pupils for growing, flourishing and developing into responsible, purposeful and wise citizens who value and respect diversity in society. It also refers to pupils' attitudes, morals and behaviour in society, developing their cultural understanding and interpersonal skills.

Summative assessment – refers to the summary of a pupil's overall learning or final achievement at the end of an academic year or at the end of a course, which involves pupils undertaking standardised tests or external examinations.

Talented – refers to those pupils who may excel in areas of the curriculum requiring visual-spatial skills or practical abilities such as sport, PE, dance, drama, music or art and design.

Thinking skills – are a series of cross-curricular higher order skills that enable pupils to understand the process of meaningful learning, how to think flexibly, and how to make reasoned judgements. It entails pupils in processing information, reasoning, enquiring, evaluating and thinking creatively.

Transfer – refers to the move from one school or phase of education to another, for example from primary school to secondary school.

Transition – refers to the move from one year group to the next within the same educational setting or school.

Well-being – means having the basic things you need to live and being healthy, safe and happy.

Useful Websites

www.antidote.org.uk

www.buildinglearningpower.co.uk

www.campaign-for-learning.org.uk

www.childrenscommissioner.org

www.circle-time.co.uk

www.classroom-assistant.com

www.everychildmatters.gov.uk

http://inclusion.ngfl.gov.uk

www.learningsupport.co.uk

www.lge.gov.uk

www.nch.org.uk/index.php

www.ofsted.gov.uk

www.rtweb.info

www.sapere.net

www.skills4schools.org.uk

www.skillsplus.gov.uk

www.tda.gov.uk

www.teachernet.gov.uk/teachingassistants

www.unhchr.ch/html/menu3/b/k2crc.htm

www.unicef.org.uk/youthvoice/wellbeing.asp

References and Further Reading

Assessment Reform Group (2002) *Assessment for Learning: 10 Principles. Research Based Principles to Guide Classroom Practice*. London: Institute of Education, University of London.

Briody, J. and McGarry, K. (2005) 'Using Social Stories to Ease Children's Transitions', in *Journal of the National Association for the Education of Young Children*, September 2005. Washington, DC: NAEYC.

Cheminais, R. (2007) *Extended Schools and Children's Centres: A Practical Guide*. London: Routledge, Taylor & Francis Group.

Children's Society, The (2006) *Good Childhood: A Question for our Times. A National Inquiry Launch Report*. London: The Children's Society.

Children's Society, The (2007) *Good Childhood: What You Told Us About Friends*. London: The Children's Society.

Cullingford, C. (1991) *The Inner World of the School*. London: Cassell.

DfES (2000) *Working with Teaching Assistants: A Good Practice Guide*. London: Department for Education and Skills.

DfES (2003) *Every Child Matters*. London: Department for Education and Skills.

DfES (2004a) *Removing Barriers to Achievement: The Government's Strategy for SEN*. London: Department for Education and Skills.

DfES (2004b) *The Five Year Strategy for Children and Learners*. London: Department for Education and Skills.

DfES (2004c) *Working Together: Giving Children and Young People a Say*. London: Department for Education and Skills.

DfES (2004d) *Every Child Matters: Next Steps*. London: Department for Education and Skills.

DfES (2004e) *Every Child Matters: Change for Children in School*. London: Department for Education and Skills.

DfES (2004f) *Pedagogy and Practice: Teaching and Learning in Secondary Schools. Teaching Repertoire. Unit 7: Questioning*. London: Department for Education and Skills.

DfES (2004g) *Pedagogy and Practice: Teaching and Learning in Secondary Schools. Creating Conditions for Learning. Unit 19: Learning Styles*. London: Department for Education and Skills.

DfES (2004h) *Excellence and Enjoyment: Learning and Teaching in the Primary Years. Creating a Learning Culture. Conditions for Learning. Professional Development Materials. Primary National Strategy.* London: Department for Education and Skills.

DfES (2004i) *Excellence and Enjoyment: Learning and Teaching in the Primary Years. Creating a Learning Culture. Classroom Community, Collaborative and Personalised Learning. Professional Development Materials. Primary National Strategy.* London: Department for Education and Skills.

DfES (2004j) *Promoting Inclusion and Tackling Underperformance: Maximising Progress: Ensuring the Attainment of Pupils with SEN. Part 1: Using Data – Target Setting and Target Getting. Key Stage 3 National Strategy.* London: Department for Education and Skills.

DfES (2004k) *Primary National Strategy, Excellence and Enjoyment: Learning and Teaching in the Primary Years. Planning and Assessment for Learning: Assessment for Learning.* London: Department for Education and Skills.

DfES (2005a) *Leading in Learning: Developing Thinking skills at Key Stage 3. Handbook for Teachers. Key Stage 3 National Strategy.* London: Department for Education and Skills.

DfES (2005b) *Leading on Inclusion: Primary National Strategy.* London: Department for Education and Skills.

DfES (2005c) *Promoting Inclusion and Tackling Underperformance: Maximising Progress: Ensuring the Attainment of Pupils with SEN. Key Stage 3 National Strategy.* London: Department for Education and Skills.

DfES (2005d) *Social and Emotional Aspects of Learning: Guidance Document. Primary National Strategy.* London: Department for Education and Skills.

DfES (2005f) *Common Core of Skills and Knowledge for the Children's Workforce.* London: Department for Education and Skills.

DfES (2005g) *Supporting the New Agenda for Children's Services and Schools: the Role of Learning Mentors and Co-ordinators. A Guide for Planners and Decision-makers in Schools and Local Authorities to Sustain and Develop Successful Provision.* London: Department for Education and Skills.

DfES (2006a) *Mentoring and Coaching CPD Capacity Building Project: National Framework for Mentoring and Coaching. Secondary National Strategy.* London: Department for Education and Skills.

DfES (2006b) *The Deployment and Impact of Support Staff in School: Report on Findings From a National Questionnaire Survey of Schools, Support Staff and Teachers (Strand 1, Wave 1, 2004).* Nottingham: Department for Education and Skills.

DfES (2006c) *Identifying Gifted and Talented Pupils: Getting Started.* Nottingham: Department for Education and Skills.

DfES (2006d) *Effective Provision for Gifted and Talented Children in Primary Education.* Nottingham: Department for Education and Skills.

DfES (2006e) *Leading on Intervention: Primary National Strategy.* London: Department for Education and Skills.

DfES (2006f) *The Five Year Strategy for Children and Learners: Maintaining the Excellent Progress*. London: Department for Education and Skills.

DfES (2006g) *Children's Workforce Strategy: Building a World-class Workforce for Children, Young People and Families. The Government's Response to the Consultation*. Nottingham: Department for Education and Skills.

DfES (2007a) *Children's Workforce Strategy: Update – Spring 2007. Building a World-class Workforce for Children, Young People and Families*. London: Department for Education and Skills.

DfES (2007b) *An Investigation of Personalised Learning: Approaches used by Schools*. Nottingham: Department for Education and Skills.

DfES and DH (2005e) *Managing Medicines in Schools and Early Years Settings*. London: Department for Education and Skills and Department of Health.

DH and DfES (2004) *Promoting Emotional Health and Well Being Through the National Healthy School Standard*. Wetherby: Health Development Agency, Department of Health/Department for Education and Skills.

DH and DfES (2005a) *National Healthy School Status: A Guide for Schools*. London: Department of Health/Department for Education and Skills.

DH and DfES (2005b) *Guidance to Healthy Schools Co-ordinators: Healthy Schools*. London: Department of Health/Department for Education and Skills.

Dryden, G. and Vos, J. (2001) *The Learning Revolution: To Change the Way the World Learns*. Stafford: Network Educational Press Limited.

Finney, M., Richards, G. and Anderson, V. (2007) 'How to Make Better Use of Teaching Assistants', in *Special Children*, 177 (27–30).

Hadfield, M. and Haw, K. (2004) 'Aspects of Voice', in *NEXUS*, Issue 2, Spring 2004, (24–25). Nottingham: National College for School Leadership.

Hargreaves, D. (2004) *Personalising Learning: Next Steps in Working Laterally*. London: Specialist Schools Trust.

Harland, J. (2004) *The Pupil Voice in School Self-evaluation*. Slough: National Foundation for Educational Research (NFER).

Hastings, S. (2003) 'The Issue: Questioning'. *Times Educational Supplement* 4 July 2003, pp. 13–16. London.

Hayward, A. (2006) *Making Inclusion Happen: A Practical Guide*. London: Paul Chapman Publishing.

Hook, P. and Vass, A. (2000a) *Confident Classroom Leadership*. London: David Fulton Publishers.

Hook, P. and Vass, A. (2000b) *Creating Winning Classrooms*. London: David Fulton Publishers.

Hopkins, B. (1999) *Restorative Justice in Schools*, unpublished. www.transformingconflict.com/aboutjustice.htm accessed 24.5.2007.

House of Commons Education and Skills Committee (2007) *Bullying: Third Report of Session 2006–07*. London: The Stationery Office.

Innocenti Research Centre (2007) *An Overview of Child Wellbeing in Rich Countries*. UNICEF.

Jackson, D. (2004) 'Why pupil voice?', in *NEXUS*, Issue 2, Spring 2004 (6–7). Nottingham: National College for School Leadership.

Jones, P. and Burns, M. (2006) *How to Transform Learning through System-wide Reform*. Stafford: Network Continuum Education.

Kamen, T. (2003) *Teaching Assistants Handbook*. London: Hodder & Stoughton.

Last, G. (2004) *Personalising Learning: Adding Value to the Learning Journey Through the Primary School*. London: Department for Education and Skills.

LGNTO (2001) *Teaching/Classroom Assistants National Occupational Standards*. London: Local Government National Training Organisation.

MacBeath, J. (2006) *School Inspection and Self-Evaluation: Working with the New Relationship*. London: Routledge, Taylor & Francis Group.

Morgan, J. (2007) *How to be a Successful Teaching Assistant*. London: Continuum.

NCH/Tesco Mobile (2005) *Putting U in the Picture: Mobile Bullying Survey*. London: National Children's Home.

NCH (2007a) *Emotional Wellbeing and Social Mobility: A New Urgency to the Debate*. NCH Briefing June 2007. London: National Children's Homes.

NCH (2007b) *Literature Review: Resilience in Children and Young People*. London: National Children's Homes.

NJCLGS (2003) *School Support Staff: The Way Forward*. London: National Joint Council for Local Government Services, Employers' Organisation for Local Government.

Ofsted (2002) *Teaching Assistants in Primary Schools: An Evaluation of the Quality and Impact of their Work*. A Report by HMI. HMI 434. London: Office for Standards in Education.

Ofsted (2003) *Bullying: Effective Action in Secondary Schools*. HMI 465. London: Office for Standards in Education.

Ofsted (2004a) *Promoting and Evaluating Pupils' Spiritual, Moral, Social and Cultural Development*. HMI 2125. London: Office for Standards in Education.

Ofsted (2004b) *Personal, Social, and Health Education in Secondary Schools*. HMI 2311. London: Office for Standards in Education.

Ofsted (2004c) *Special Educational Needs and Disability: Towards Inclusive Schools*. HMI 2276. London: Office for Standards in Education.

Ofsted (2005a) *Every Child Matters: Framework for the Inspection of Schools*. London: Office for Standards in Education.

Ofsted (2005b) *Healthy Minds: Promoting Emotional Health and Well-being in Schools*. HMI 2450. London: Office for Standards in Education.

Ofsted (2005c) *Self Evaluation form for Secondary Schools (with or without Sixth Forms)*. London: Office for Standards in Education.

Ofsted (2006a) *Healthy Eating in Schools*. HMI 2625. London: Office for Standards in Education.

Ofsted (2006b) *Improving Performance Through School Self-evaluation and Improvement Planning: Further Guidance*. London: Office for Standards in Education.

Ofsted (2006c) *Best Practice in Self-evaluation: A Survey of Schools, Colleges and Local Authorities*. London: Office for Standards in Education.

Ofsted (2006d) *Healthy Schools, Healthy Children? The Contribution of Education to Pupils' Health and Well-being*. HMI 2563. London: Office for Standards in Education.

Ofsted (2006e) *Inclusion: Does it Matter Where Pupils are Taught? Provision and Outcomes in Different Settings for Pupils with Learning Difficulties and Disabilities*. HMI 2535. London: Office for Standards in Education.

Ofsted (2006f) *Inspection Matters, Issue 11, B3 Questions about ECM Outcomes for Possible Consideration during an Inspection*. London: Office for Standards in Education.

Ofsted (2006g) *Using the Evaluation Schedule: Guidance for Inspectors of Schools*. London: Office for Standards in Education.

Ofsted (2007a) *Guidance on Gathering Evidence for Every Child Matters Outcomes in Section 162A Inspections*. London: Office for Standards in Education.

Ofsted (2007b) *Time for Change? Personal, Social and Health Education*. London: Office for Standards in Education.

Ofsted (2007c) *Inspection Matters 16, Evaluating the Standard of Learners' Behaviour*. London: Office for Standards in Education.

Overall, L. (2007) *Supporting Children's Learning: A Guide for Teaching Assistants*. London: SAGE Publications.

Palmer, S. (2006) *Toxic Childhood: How the Modern World is Damaging our Children and what we can do about it*. London: Orion.

Pease, A. and Pease, B. (2001) *Why Men don't Listen and Women can't Read Maps*. London: Orion Books Limited.

Reid, G. (2005) *Learning Styles and Inclusion*. London: Paul Chapman Publishing.

Rudduck, J. and Flutter, J. (2006) *Consulting Young People in Schools*. Cambridge: Economic and Social Research Council.

School Councils UK (2006) *School Councils UK Briefing: School Councils and Every Child Matters*. London: School Councils UK.

Smith, A. (2001) *Reaching out to all Learners*. Stafford: Network Educational Press.

Smith, A. and Call, N. (1999) *The Alps Approach: Accelerated Learning in Primary Schools*. Stafford: Network Educational Press Limited.

Smith, J. (2007) 'Questioning', in *Gifted & Talented UPDATE*, Issue 47 (p10). London: Optimus Education.

TDA (2005) *Building the School Team: Our Plans for Support Staff Development 2005–06. Frequently Asked Questions.* London: Training and Development Agency for Schools.

TDA (2006a) *Developing People to Support Learning: A Skills Strategy for the Wider School Workforce 2006–09.* London: Training and Development Agency for Schools.

TDA (2006b) *Career Development Framework for School Support Staff: Guidance February 2006.* London: Training and Development Agency for Schools.

TDA (2006c) *Issues Addressed from First Stakeholder Consultation.* London: Training and Development Agency for Schools.

TDA (2006d) *Draft National Occupational Standards for Supporting Teaching and Learning in the Classroom.* London: Training and Development Agency for Schools.

TDA (2006e) *Teaching Assistant Standards Consultation on TA/CA National Occupational Standards.* London: Training and Development Agency for Schools.

TDA (2006f) *Primary Induction: Role and Context. For Teaching Assistant Trainers.* London: Training and Development Agency for Schools.

TDA (2007) *National Occupational Standards for Supporting Teaching and Learning in Schools.* London: Training and Development Agency for Schools.

Teaching and Learning in 2020 Review Group (2006) *2020 Vision: Report of the Teaching and Learning in 2020 Review Group.* London: DfES.

Teare, B. (2006) *Successful Provision for Able and Talented Children.* London: Network Continuum Education.

TLRP/ESRC (2004) *Personalised Learning: A Commentary by the Teaching and Learning Research Programme.* Cambridge: Teaching and Learning Programme/Economic and Social Research Council.

United Nations (1989) *Convention on the Rights of the Child.* UN General Assembly Document A/RES/44/25. New York: United Nations.

W3 Insights (2005) *Pupil Attitudes to Self and School (PASS).* Wolverhampton: W3 Insights Limited.

West-Burnham, J. and Coates, M. (2005) *Personalizing Learning: Transforming Education for Every Child.* Stafford: Network Educational Press.

Wilmot, E. (2006) *Personalising Learning in the Primary Classroom: A Practical Guide for Teachers and School Leaders.* Bancyfelin, Carmarthen: Crown House Publishing Limited.

Index

Tables are indicated by italic page numbers, figures by bold.

eBooks – at www.eBookstore.tandf.co.uk

A library at your fingertips!

eBooks are electronic versions of printed books. You can store them on your PC/laptop or browse them online.

They have advantages for anyone needing rapid access to a wide variety of published, copyright information.

eBooks can help your research by enabling you to bookmark chapters, annotate text and use instant searches to find specific words or phrases. Several eBook files would fit on even a small laptop or PDA.

NEW: Save money by eSubscribing: cheap, online access to any eBook for as long as you need it.

Annual subscription packages

We now offer special low-cost bulk subscriptions to packages of eBooks in certain subject areas. These are available to libraries or to individuals.

For more information please contact webmaster.ebooks@tandf.co.uk

We're continually developing the eBook concept, so keep up to date by visiting the website.

www.eBookstore.tandf.co.uk